TEACHER'S PET PUBLICATIONS

PUZZLE PACK
for
Our Town

based on the play by
Thornton Wilder

Written by
William T. Collins

© 2005 Teacher's Pet Publications
All Rights Reserved

The materials in this packet are copyrighted
by Teacher's Pet Publications, Inc.

These pages may be duplicated by the purchaser
for use in the purchaser's own classroom.

Copying any of these materials and distributing them
for any other purpose is a violation of the copyright laws.

© 2005 Teacher's Pet Publications, Inc.
www.tpet.com

INTRODUCTION
If you already own the LitPlan for this title, this Puzzle Pack will refresh your Unit Resource Materials and Vocabulary Resource Materials sections plus give you additional materials you can substitute into the tests. If you do not already have a complete LitPlan, these pages will give you some supplemental materials to use with your own plan. There are two main groups of materials: one set for unit words (such as characters' names, symbols, places, etc.) and one set for vocabulary words associated with the book.

WORD LIST
There is a word list for both the unit words and the vocabulary words. These lists show you which words are being used in the materials and the clues or definitions being used for those words. You may want to give students a word list with clues/definitions to help them, or you may want students to only have a word list (without clues/definitions) if you want them to work a little harder. Both are available for duplication. The word lists can also be your "calling key" for the bingo games.

FILL IN THE BLANK AND MATCHING
There are 4 each of the fill in the blank and matching worksheets for both the unit and vocabulary words. These pages can be used either as extra worksheets for students or as objective parts of a unit test. They can be done individually if students need extra help or as a whole class activity to review the material covered.

MAGIC SQUARES
The magic squares not only reinforce the material covered but also work on reasoning and math skills. Many teachers have told us that their students really enjoy doing these!

WORD SEARCH PUZZLES
The word search words go in all directions, as indicated on your answer keys. Two of the word search puzzles have the clues listed rather than the words. This makes the puzzle a little more difficult, but it reinforces the material better. Two word search puzzles have words only for students who find the clue puzzles too difficult.

CROSSWORD PUZZLES
Both unit and vocabulary word sections have 4 crossword puzzles.

BINGO CARDS
There are 32 individual bingo cards for the unit words and 32 individual bingo cards for the vocabulary words. You can use your word list as a "call list," calling the words at random and marking them off of your list as you go, or you could use the flash cards by cutting them apart and drawing the words at random from a hat (or box or whatever). To make a better review, you might ask for the definition and spelling of each word as you call it out–or you could call out the definitions and have students tell you the words they need to look for on the puzzle.

JUGGLE LETTERS
The vocabulary juggle letter game is intended to help students learn the spellings of the words. One sheet has the definitions listed on it as an extra help for students who need it or to reinforce the definitions if you choose to do so.

FLASH CARDS
We've included a set of vocabulary flash cards you can duplicate, cut, and fold for your students. Some teachers make a few sets for general use by the class; others make a set for each student. Some teachers duplicate them for each student and have the students cut & fold their own. You can cut out just the words and put them in a hat, have each student pick out one word and write the definition and a sentence for that word. Students then swap words and papers, with the next student adding a sentence of his own under the last one. You can have students swap as many times as you like. Each time the student will read the sentences written prior to his own and then add a sentence. You can cut out the words and definitions separately and play "I Have; Who Has?" Each student in the room draws a word and definition. The first student says, "I have (the name of the word). Who has the definition?" The student with the definition reads it then says, "I have (the name of the vocabulary word she has). Who has the definition?" The round continues until all words and definitions have been given.

Our Town Word List

No.	Word	Clue/Definition
1.	ACT	Play division
2.	APPENDIX	Wally Webb's burst
3.	CEMETERY	Setting for most of Act III
4.	CHILDBIRTH	Emily died during this
5.	CORNERS	Grover's ___
6.	CRIED	What the ladies did at the wedding
7.	CROWELL	He delivers newspapers
8.	DEATH	The end of one's life
9.	DOCTOR	Mr. Gibbs is one
10.	EARTH	'Oh, ___, you are too wonderful for anybody to realize you!'
11.	EDITOR	Mr. Webb's occupation
12.	EMILY	She married George.
13.	FUNERAL	Burial ceremony
14.	GEORGE	Rebecca's brother
15.	GIBBS	Rebecca's last name
16.	LEAST	'Choose the ___ important day of your life; it will be important enough.'
17.	LIFE	'You've got to love ___ to have ___.'
18.	MANAGER	Stage ___ gives the audience background information
19.	MOON	George & Rebecca talk about it before going to sleep.
20.	NEWSOME	Milk man
21.	ORDINARY	Not unusual; routine
22.	PNEUMONIA	Mr. Gibbs died of it.
23.	SAM	Craig; Mrs. Gibbs's nephew
24.	SCENE	Act division
25.	SOAMES	Gossipy choir member
26.	STIMSON	His drinking problem is a scandal.
27.	TOWN	Our ___
28.	TROUBLES	Everyone has a right to their own
29.	WEDDING	Marriage ceremony
30.	WILDER	Author

Copyrighted

Our Town Fill In The Blanks 1

1. Craig; Mrs. Gibbs's nephew
2. Act division
3. She married George.
4. He delivers newspapers
5. Mr. Gibbs is one
6. Everyone has a right to their own
7. 'Choose the ___ important day of your life; it will be important enough.'
8. Mr. Webb's occupation
9. Rebecca's last name
10. Mr. Gibbs died of it.
11. What the ladies did at the wedding
12. 'You've got to love ___ to have ___.'
13. Gossipy choir member
14. Milk man
15. Not unusual; routine
16. Setting for most of Act III
17. Emily died during this
18. George & Rebecca talk about it before going to sleep.
19. Our ___
20. Wally Webb's burst

Our Town Fill In The Blanks 1 Answer Key

SAM	1. Craig; Mrs. Gibbs's nephew
SCENE	2. Act division
EMILY	3. She married George.
CROWELL	4. He delivers newspapers
DOCTOR	5. Mr. Gibbs is one
TROUBLES	6. Everyone has a right to their own
LEAST	7. 'Choose the ___ important day of your life; it will be important enough.'
EDITOR	8. Mr. Webb's occupation
GIBBS	9. Rebecca's last name
PNEUMONIA	10. Mr. Gibbs died of it.
CRIED	11. What the ladies did at the wedding
LIFE	12. 'You've got to love ___ to have ___.'
SOAMES	13. Gossipy choir member
NEWSOME	14. Milk man
ORDINARY	15. Not unusual; routine
CEMETERY	16. Setting for most of Act III
CHILDBIRTH	17. Emily died during this
MOON	18. George & Rebecca talk about it before going to sleep.
TOWN	19. Our ___
APPENDIX	20. Wally Webb's burst

Copyrighted

Our Town Fill In The Blanks 2

_____

1. Mr. Gibbs is one

2. Everyone has a right to their own

3. Mr. Gibbs died of it.

4. His drinking problem is a scandal.

5. The end of one's life

6. He delivers newspapers

7. Act division

8. 'You've got to love ___ to have ___.'

9. Stage ___ gives the audience background information

10. 'Choose the ___ important day of your life; it will be important enough.'

11. Burial ceremony

12. What the ladies did at the wedding

13. Rebecca's last name

14. Gossipy choir member

15. Author

16. Grover's ___

17. Not unusual; routine

18. Our ___

19. Mr. Webb's occupation

20. George & Rebecca talk about it before going to sleep.

Our Town Fill In The Blanks 2 Answer Key

DOCTOR	1. Mr. Gibbs is one
TROUBLES	2. Everyone has a right to their own
PNEUMONIA	3. Mr. Gibbs died of it.
STIMSON	4. His drinking problem is a scandal.
DEATH	5. The end of one's life
CROWELL	6. He delivers newspapers
SCENE	7. Act division
LIFE	8. 'You've got to love ___ to have ___.'
MANAGER	9. Stage ___ gives the audience background information
LEAST	10. 'Choose the ___ important day of your life; it will be important enough.'
FUNERAL	11. Burial ceremony
CRIED	12. What the ladies did at the wedding
GIBBS	13. Rebecca's last name
SOAMES	14. Gossipy choir member
WILDER	15. Author
CORNERS	16. Grover's ___
ORDINARY	17. Not unusual; routine
TOWN	18. Our ___
EDITOR	19. Mr. Webb's occupation
MOON	20. George & Rebecca talk about it before going to sleep.

Our Town Fill In The Blanks 3

_____

1. Act division
2. Marriage ceremony
3. Author
4. Mr. Gibbs died of it.
5. Not unusual; routine
6. Stage ___ gives the audience background information
7. Grover's ___
8. He delivers newspapers
9. Rebecca's brother
10. Emily died during this
11. 'Oh, ___, you are too wonderful for anybody to realize you!'
12. Gossipy choir member
13. His drinking problem is a scandal.
14. Rebecca's last name
15. What the ladies did at the wedding
16. Milk man
17. Burial ceremony
18. 'Choose the ___ important day of your life; it will be important enough.'
19. Everyone has a right to their own
20. The end of one's life

Our Town Fill In The Blanks 3 Answer Key

SCENE	1. Act division
WEDDING	2. Marriage ceremony
WILDER	3. Author
PNEUMONIA	4. Mr. Gibbs died of it.
ORDINARY	5. Not unusual; routine
MANAGER	6. Stage ___ gives the audience background information
CORNERS	7. Grover's ___
CROWELL	8. He delivers newspapers
GEORGE	9. Rebecca's brother
CHILDBIRTH	10. Emily died during this
EARTH	11. 'Oh, ___, you are too wonderful for anybody to realize you!'
SOAMES	12. Gossipy choir member
STIMSON	13. His drinking problem is a scandal.
GIBBS	14. Rebecca's last name
CRIED	15. What the ladies did at the wedding
NEWSOME	16. Milk man
FUNERAL	17. Burial ceremony
LEAST	18. 'Choose the ___ important day of your life; it will be important enough.'
TROUBLES	19. Everyone has a right to their own
DEATH	20. The end of one's life

Our Town Fill In The Blanks 4

_____ 1. Rebecca's last name

_____ 2. The end of one's life

_____ 3. Play division

_____ 4. Craig; Mrs. Gibbs's nephew

_____ 5. His drinking problem is a scandal.

_____ 6. 'Oh, ___, you are too wonderful for anybody to realize you!'

_____ 7. 'Choose the ___ important day of your life; it will be important enough.'

_____ 8. Mr. Webb's occupation

_____ 9. What the ladies did at the wedding

_____ 10. George & Rebecca talk about it before going to sleep.

_____ 11. Our ___

_____ 12. Emily died during this

_____ 13. He delivers newspapers

_____ 14. Author

_____ 15. Burial ceremony

_____ 16. Everyone has a right to their own

_____ 17. Mr. Gibbs is one

_____ 18. Setting for most of Act III

_____ 19. Gossipy choir member

_____ 20. Rebecca's brother

Our Town Fill In The Blanks 4 Answer Key

Answer	#	Clue
GIBBS	1.	Rebecca's last name
DEATH	2.	The end of one's life
ACT	3.	Play division
SAM	4.	Craig; Mrs. Gibbs's nephew
STIMSON	5.	His drinking problem is a scandal.
EARTH	6.	'Oh, ___, you are too wonderful for anybody to realize you!'
LEAST	7.	'Choose the ___ important day of your life; it will be important enough.'
EDITOR	8.	Mr. Webb's occupation
CRIED	9.	What the ladies did at the wedding
MOON	10.	George & Rebecca talk about it before going to sleep.
TOWN	11.	Our ___
CHILDBIRTH	12.	Emily died during this
CROWELL	13.	He delivers newspapers
WILDER	14.	Author
FUNERAL	15.	Burial ceremony
TROUBLES	16.	Everyone has a right to their own
DOCTOR	17.	Mr. Gibbs is one
CEMETERY	18.	Setting for most of Act III
SOAMES	19.	Gossipy choir member
GEORGE	20.	Rebecca's brother

Our Town Matching 1

___ 1. CORNERS   A. Grover's ___
___ 2. WILDER   B. Not unusual; routine
___ 3. SCENE   C. The end of one's life
___ 4. TOWN   D. Our ___
___ 5. ACT   E. Wally Webb's burst
___ 6. GIBBS   F. Burial ceremony
___ 7. CROWELL   G. Author
___ 8. NEWSOME   H. Gossipy choir member
___ 9. EMILY   I. Mr. Gibbs died of it.
___ 10. TROUBLES   J. 'Choose the ___ important day of your life; it will be important enough.'
___ 11. FUNERAL   K. 'You've got to love ___ to have ___.'
___ 12. STIMSON   L. Act division
___ 13. APPENDIX   M. Play division
___ 14. GEORGE   N. Setting for most of Act III
___ 15. MANAGER   O. Marriage ceremony
___ 16. ORDINARY   P. Stage ___ gives the audience background information
___ 17. SOAMES   Q. Everyone has a right to their own
___ 18. WEDDING   R. Emily died during this
___ 19. DEATH   S. His drinking problem is a scandal.
___ 20. CRIED   T. He delivers newspapers
___ 21. CHILDBIRTH   U. Milk man
___ 22. PNEUMONIA   V. Rebecca's brother
___ 23. LEAST   W. She married George.
___ 24. CEMETERY   X. What the ladies did at the wedding
___ 25. LIFE   Y. Rebecca's last name

Our Town Matching 1 Answer Key

A - 1.	CORNERS	A. Grover's ___
G - 2.	WILDER	B. Not unusual; routine
L - 3.	SCENE	C. The end of one's life
D - 4.	TOWN	D. Our ___
M - 5.	ACT	E. Wally Webb's burst
Y - 6.	GIBBS	F. Burial ceremony
T - 7.	CROWELL	G. Author
U - 8.	NEWSOME	H. Gossipy choir member
W - 9.	EMILY	I. Mr. Gibbs died of it.
Q - 10.	TROUBLES	J. 'Choose the ___ important day of your life; it will be important enough.'
F - 11.	FUNERAL	K. 'You've got to love ___ to have ___.'
S - 12.	STIMSON	L. Act division
E - 13.	APPENDIX	M. Play division
V - 14.	GEORGE	N. Setting for most of Act III
P - 15.	MANAGER	O. Marriage ceremony
B - 16.	ORDINARY	P. Stage ___ gives the audience background information
H - 17.	SOAMES	Q. Everyone has a right to their own
O - 18.	WEDDING	R. Emily died during this
C - 19.	DEATH	S. His drinking problem is a scandal.
X - 20.	CRIED	T. He delivers newspapers
R - 21.	CHILDBIRTH	U. Milk man
I - 22.	PNEUMONIA	V. Rebecca's brother
J - 23.	LEAST	W. She married George.
N - 24.	CEMETERY	X. What the ladies did at the wedding
K - 25.	LIFE	Y. Rebecca's last name

Our Town Matching 2

___ 1. GIBBS   A. Rebecca's last name
___ 2. SAM   B. His drinking problem is a scandal.
___ 3. DEATH   C. Author
___ 4. PNEUMONIA   D. What the ladies did at the wedding
___ 5. CEMETERY   E. The end of one's life
___ 6. MANAGER   F. Our ___
___ 7. WILDER   G. Wally Webb's burst
___ 8. SOAMES   H. 'You've got to love ___ to have ___.'
___ 9. SCENE   I. 'Oh, ___, you are too wonderful for anybody to realize you!'
___10. FUNERAL   J. Setting for most of Act III
___11. CROWELL   K. Milk man
___12. NEWSOME   L. Mr. Webb's occupation
___13. EDITOR   M. Gossipy choir member
___14. MOON   N. Everyone has a right to their own
___15. ORDINARY   O. Act division
___16. LEAST   P. 'Choose the ___ important day of your life; it will be important enough.'
___17. CRIED   Q. Play division
___18. ACT   R. Craig; Mrs. Gibbs's nephew
___19. APPENDIX   S. He delivers newspapers
___20. STIMSON   T. Emily died during this
___21. TOWN   U. Stage ___ gives the audience background information
___22. TROUBLES   V. Burial ceremony
___23. CHILDBIRTH   W. Mr. Gibbs died of it.
___24. EARTH   X. George & Rebecca talk about it before going to sleep.
___25. LIFE   Y. Not unusual; routine

Our Town Matching 2 Answer Key

A - 1. GIBBS	A.	Rebecca's last name
R - 2. SAM	B.	His drinking problem is a scandal.
E - 3. DEATH	C.	Author
W - 4. PNEUMONIA	D.	What the ladies did at the wedding
J - 5. CEMETERY	E.	The end of one's life
U - 6. MANAGER	F.	Our ___
C - 7. WILDER	G.	Wally Webb's burst
M - 8. SOAMES	H.	'You've got to love ___ to have ___.'
O - 9. SCENE	I.	'Oh, ___, you are too wonderful for anybody to realize you!'
V - 10. FUNERAL	J.	Setting for most of Act III
S - 11. CROWELL	K.	Milk man
K - 12. NEWSOME	L.	Mr. Webb's occupation
L - 13. EDITOR	M.	Gossipy choir member
X - 14. MOON	N.	Everyone has a right to their own
Y - 15. ORDINARY	O.	Act division
P - 16. LEAST	P.	'Choose the ___ important day of your life; it will be important enough.'
D - 17. CRIED	Q.	Play division
Q - 18. ACT	R.	Craig; Mrs. Gibbs's nephew
G - 19. APPENDIX	S.	He delivers newspapers
B - 20. STIMSON	T.	Emily died during this
F - 21. TOWN	U.	Stage ___ gives the audience background information
N - 22. TROUBLES	V.	Burial ceremony
T - 23. CHILDBIRTH	W.	Mr. Gibbs died of it.
I - 24. EARTH	X.	George & Rebecca talk about it before going to sleep.
H - 25. LIFE	Y.	Not unusual; routine

Our Town Matching 3

___ 1. APPENDIX   A. He delivers newspapers
___ 2. CRIED   B. Everyone has a right to their own
___ 3. CORNERS   C. Grover's ___
___ 4. EARTH   D. The end of one's life
___ 5. MANAGER   E. What the ladies did at the wedding
___ 6. ACT   F. His drinking problem is a scandal.
___ 7. SCENE   G. 'Choose the ___ important day of your life; it will be important enough.'
___ 8. DOCTOR   H. Setting for most of Act III
___ 9. PNEUMONIA   I. Author
___10. NEWSOME   J. Marriage ceremony
___11. STIMSON   K. Rebecca's last name
___12. EDITOR   L. Burial ceremony
___13. TROUBLES   M. Mr. Gibbs is one
___14. DEATH   N. Play division
___15. CEMETERY   O. Milk man
___16. GEORGE   P. Mr. Webb's occupation
___17. CROWELL   Q. Act division
___18. MOON   R. Not unusual; routine
___19. CHILDBIRTH   S. Stage ___ gives the audience background information
___20. WILDER   T. Mr. Gibbs died of it.
___21. FUNERAL   U. Rebecca's brother
___22. ORDINARY   V. Emily died during this
___23. WEDDING   W. 'Oh, ___, you are too wonderful for anybody to realize you!'
___24. GIBBS   X. George & Rebecca talk about it before going to sleep.
___25. LEAST   Y. Wally Webb's burst

Our Town Matching 3 Answer Key

Y - 1.	APPENDIX	A.	He delivers newspapers
E - 2.	CRIED	B.	Everyone has a right to their own
C - 3.	CORNERS	C.	Grover's ___
W - 4.	EARTH	D.	The end of one's life
S - 5.	MANAGER	E.	What the ladies did at the wedding
N - 6.	ACT	F.	His drinking problem is a scandal.
Q - 7.	SCENE	G.	'Choose the ___ important day of your life; it will be important enough.'
M - 8.	DOCTOR	H.	Setting for most of Act III
T - 9.	PNEUMONIA	I.	Author
O -10.	NEWSOME	J.	Marriage ceremony
F -11.	STIMSON	K.	Rebecca's last name
P -12.	EDITOR	L.	Burial ceremony
B -13.	TROUBLES	M.	Mr. Gibbs is one
D -14.	DEATH	N.	Play division
H -15.	CEMETERY	O.	Milk man
U -16.	GEORGE	P.	Mr. Webb's occupation
A -17.	CROWELL	Q.	Act division
X -18.	MOON	R.	Not unusual; routine
V -19.	CHILDBIRTH	S.	Stage ___ gives the audience background information
I - 20.	WILDER	T.	Mr. Gibbs died of it.
L -21.	FUNERAL	U.	Rebecca's brother
R -22.	ORDINARY	V.	Emily died during this
J - 23.	WEDDING	W.	'Oh, ___, you are too wonderful for anybody to realize you!'
K -24.	GIBBS	X.	George & Rebecca talk about it before going to sleep.
G -25.	LEAST	Y.	Wally Webb's burst

Our Town Matching 4

___ 1. SOAMES   A. Setting for most of Act III
___ 2. TOWN   B. Gossipy choir member
___ 3. EARTH   C. Wally Webb's burst
___ 4. GEORGE   D. Marriage ceremony
___ 5. ORDINARY   E. He delivers newspapers
___ 6. CEMETERY   F. 'Choose the ___ important day of your life; it will be important enough.'
___ 7. EMILY   G. Emily died during this
___ 8. FUNERAL   H. She married George.
___ 9. EDITOR   I. 'You've got to love ___ to have ___.'
___10. SAM   J. Mr. Gibbs is one
___11. SCENE   K. Author
___12. WEDDING   L. George & Rebecca talk about it before going to sleep.
___13. GIBBS   M. Rebecca's brother
___14. CROWELL   N. Our ___
___15. WILDER   O. Mr. Webb's occupation
___16. LEAST   P. The end of one's life
___17. CRIED   Q. Act division
___18. MOON   R. Not unusual; routine
___19. DEATH   S. His drinking problem is a scandal.
___20. ACT   T. Burial ceremony
___21. CHILDBIRTH U. 'Oh, ___, you are too wonderful for anybody to realize you!'
___22. LIFE   V. Craig; Mrs. Gibbs's nephew
___23. STIMSON   W. Rebecca's last name
___24. APPENDIX   X. What the ladies did at the wedding
___25. DOCTOR   Y. Play division

Our Town Matching 4 Answer Key

B - 1. SOAMES	A.	Setting for most of Act III
N - 2. TOWN	B.	Gossipy choir member
U - 3. EARTH	C.	Wally Webb's burst
M - 4. GEORGE	D.	Marriage ceremony
R - 5. ORDINARY	E.	He delivers newspapers
A - 6. CEMETERY	F.	'Choose the ___ important day of your life; it will be important enough.'
H - 7. EMILY	G.	Emily died during this
T - 8. FUNERAL	H.	She married George.
O - 9. EDITOR	I.	'You've got to love ___ to have ___.'
V -10. SAM	J.	Mr. Gibbs is one
Q -11. SCENE	K.	Author
D -12. WEDDING	L.	George & Rebecca talk about it before going to sleep.
W -13. GIBBS	M.	Rebecca's brother
E -14. CROWELL	N.	Our ___
K -15. WILDER	O.	Mr. Webb's occupation
F -16. LEAST	P.	The end of one's life
X -17. CRIED	Q.	Act division
L -18. MOON	R.	Not unusual; routine
P -19. DEATH	S.	His drinking problem is a scandal.
Y -20. ACT	T.	Burial ceremony
G -21. CHILDBIRTH	U.	'Oh, ___, you are too wonderful for anybody to realize you!'
I -22. LIFE	V.	Craig; Mrs. Gibbs's nephew
S -23. STIMSON	W.	Rebecca's last name
C -24. APPENDIX	X.	What the ladies did at the wedding
J -25. DOCTOR	Y.	Play division

Our Town Magic Squares 1

Match the definition with the vocabulary word. Put your answers in the magic squares below. When your answers are correct, all columns and rows will add to the same number.

A. TROUBLES E. SAM   I. EMILY   M. CRIED
B. CORNERS   F. CEMETERY J. ACT   N. LEAST
C. GIBBS   G. DOCTOR   K. SOAMES   O. EDITOR
D. STIMSON   H. MANAGER   L. APPENDIX P. FUNERAL

1. Rebecca's last name
2. Play division
3. Setting for most of Act III
4. Mr. Webb's occupation
5. Burial ceremony
6. Craig; Mrs. Gibbs's nephew
7. She married George.
8. His drinking problem is a scandal.
9. What the ladies did at the wedding
10. Stage ___ gives the audience background information
11. Wally Webb's burst
12. Everyone has a right to their own
13. Grover's ___
14. Gossipy choir member
15. Mr. Gibbs is one
16. 'Choose the ___ important day of your life; it will be important enough.'

A=	B=	C=	D=
E=	F=	G=	H=
I=	J=	K=	L=
M=	N=	O=	P=

Our Town Magic Squares 1 Answer Key

Match the definition with the vocabulary word. Put your answers in the magic squares below. When your answers are correct, all columns and rows will add to the same number.

A. TROUBLES E. SAM I. EMILY M. CRIED
B. CORNERS F. CEMETERY J. ACT N. LEAST
C. GIBBS G. DOCTOR K. SOAMES O. EDITOR
D. STIMSON H. MANAGER L. APPENDIX P. FUNERAL

1. Rebecca's last name
2. Play division
3. Setting for most of Act III
4. Mr. Webb's occupation
5. Burial ceremony
6. Craig; Mrs. Gibbs's nephew
7. She married George.
8. His drinking problem is a scandal.
9. What the ladies did at the wedding
10. Stage ___ gives the audience background information
11. Wally Webb's burst
12. Everyone has a right to their own
13. Grover's ___
14. Gossipy choir member
15. Mr. Gibbs is one
16. 'Choose the ___ important day of your life; it will be important enough.'

A=12	B=13	C=1	D=8
E=6	F=3	G=15	H=10
I=7	J=2	K=14	L=11
M=9	N=16	O=4	P=5

Our Town Magic Squares 2

Match the definition with the vocabulary word. Put your answers in the magic squares below. When your answers are correct, all columns and rows will add to the same number.

A. ACT
B. SAM
C. CORNERS
D. EDITOR
E. CROWELL
F. TROUBLES
G. DOCTOR
H. PNEUMONIA
I. EARTH
J. TOWN
K. FUNERAL
L. EMILY
M. CHILDBIRTH
N. SCENE
O. WEDDING
P. LIFE

1. Everyone has a right to their own
2. 'Oh, ___, you are too wonderful for anybody to realize you!'
3. Marriage ceremony
4. Mr. Webb's occupation
5. Emily died during this
6. Craig; Mrs. Gibbs's nephew
7. Mr. Gibbs died of it.
8. Burial ceremony
9. Grover's ___
10. 'You've got to love ___ to have ___.'
11. Our ___
12. He delivers newspapers
13. She married George.
14. Mr. Gibbs is one
15. Play division
16. Act division

A=	B=	C=	D=
E=	F=	G=	H=
I=	J=	K=	L=
M=	N=	O=	P=

Our Town Magic Squares 2 Answer Key

Match the definition with the vocabulary word. Put your answers in the magic squares below. When your answers are correct, all columns and rows will add to the same number.

A. ACT
B. SAM
C. CORNERS
D. EDITOR
E. CROWELL
F. TROUBLES
G. DOCTOR
H. PNEUMONIA
I. EARTH
J. TOWN
K. FUNERAL
L. EMILY
M. CHILDBIRTH
N. SCENE
O. WEDDING
P. LIFE

1. Everyone has a right to their own ___
2. 'Oh, ___, you are too wonderful for anybody to realize you!'
3. Marriage ceremony
4. Mr. Webb's occupation
5. Emily died during this
6. Craig; Mrs. Gibbs's nephew
7. Mr. Gibbs died of it.
8. Burial ceremony
9. Grover's ___
10. 'You've got to love ___ to have ___.'
11. Our ___
12. He delivers newspapers
13. She married George.
14. Mr. Gibbs is one
15. Play division
16. Act division

A=15	B=6	C=9	D=4
E=12	F=1	G=14	H=7
I=2	J=11	K=8	L=13
M=5	N=16	O=3	P=10

Our Town Magic Squares 3

Match the definition with the vocabulary word. Put your answers in the magic squares below. When your answers are correct, all columns and rows will add to the same number.

A. CHILDBIRTH   E. DOCTOR   I. LIFE   M. ACT
B. APPENDIX   F. ORDINARY   J. DEATH   N. MOON
C. GEORGE   G. SAM   K. CROWELL   O. TOWN
D. CRIED   H. GIBBS   L. CORNERS   P. WILDER

1. Emily died during this
2. George & Rebecca talk about it before going to sleep.
3. The end of one's life
4. Mr. Gibbs is one
5. Craig; Mrs. Gibbs's nephew
6. Grover's ___
7. Author
8. Rebecca's brother
9. Our ___
10. What the ladies did at the wedding
11. Rebecca's last name
12. He delivers newspapers
13. 'You've got to love ___ to have ___.'
14. Not unusual; routine
15. Wally Webb's burst
16. Play division

A=	B=	C=	D=
E=	F=	G=	H=
I=	J=	K=	L=
M=	N=	O=	P=

Our Town Magic Squares 3 Answer Key

Match the definition with the vocabulary word. Put your answers in the magic squares below. When your answers are correct, all columns and rows will add to the same number.

A. CHILDBIRTH   E. DOCTOR   I. LIFE   M. ACT
B. APPENDIX   F. ORDINARY   J. DEATH   N. MOON
C. GEORGE   G. SAM   K. CROWELL   O. TOWN
D. CRIED   H. GIBBS   L. CORNERS   P. WILDER

1. Emily died during this
2. George & Rebecca talk about it before going to sleep.
3. The end of one's life
4. Mr. Gibbs is one
5. Craig; Mrs. Gibbs's nephew
6. Grover's ___
7. Author
8. Rebecca's brother
9. Our ___
10. What the ladies did at the wedding
11. Rebecca's last name
12. He delivers newspapers
13. 'You've got to love ___ to have ___.'
14. Not unusual; routine
15. Wally Webb's burst
16. Play division

A=1	B=15	C=8	D=10
E=4	F=14	G=5	H=11
I=13	J=3	K=12	L=6
M=16	N=2	O=9	P=7

Our Town Magic Squares 4

Match the definition with the vocabulary word. Put your answers in the magic squares below. When your answers are correct, all columns and rows will add to the same number.

A. LEAST
B. SCENE
C. MANAGER
D. LIFE
E. EMILY
F. CROWELL
G. ORDINARY
H. FUNERAL
I. APPENDIX
J. EDITOR
K. CORNERS
L. CEMETERY
M. NEWSOME
N. GEORGE
O. TOWN
P. PNEUMONIA

1. Milk man
2. He delivers newspapers
3. Burial ceremony
4. Our ___
5. Setting for most of Act III
6. Stage ___ gives the audience background information
7. 'Choose the ___ important day of your life; it will be important enough.'
8. Mr. Webb's occupation
9. Grover's ___
10. 'You've got to love ___ to have ___.'
11. Act division
12. Wally Webb's burst
13. Rebecca's brother
14. She married George.
15. Not unusual; routine
16. Mr. Gibbs died of it.

A=	B=	C=	D=
E=	F=	G=	H=
I=	J=	K=	L=
M=	N=	O=	P=

Our Town Magic Squares 4 Answer Key

Match the definition with the vocabulary word. Put your answers in the magic squares below. When your answers are correct, all columns and rows will add to the same number.

A. LEAST   E. EMILY   I. APPENDIX   M. NEWSOME
B. SCENE   F. CROWELL   J. EDITOR   N. GEORGE
C. MANAGER   G. ORDINARY   K. CORNERS   O. TOWN
D. LIFE   H. FUNERAL   L. CEMETERY   P. PNEUMONIA

1. Milk man
2. He delivers newspapers
3. Burial ceremony
4. Our ___
5. Setting for most of Act III
6. Stage ___ gives the audience background information
7. 'Choose the ___ important day of your life; it will be important enough.'
8. Mr. Webb's occupation
9. Grover's ___
10. 'You've got to love ___ to have ___.'
11. Act division
12. Wally Webb's burst
13. Rebecca's brother
14. She married George.
15. Not unusual; routine
16. Mr. Gibbs died of it.

A=7	B=11	C=6	D=10
E=14	F=2	G=15	H=3
I=12	J=8	K=9	L=5
M=1	N=13	O=4	P=16

Our Town Word Search 1

Words are placed backwards, forward, diagonally, up and down. Clues listed below can help you find the words. Circle the hidden vocabulary words in the maze.

```
S F M F Z M H S N N N L V W Y R X R
Z C D D W A B D S L E M J V R S D J
F G O F M N J S Z N W P B Y E N Q C
S L X R J A C X T N S Y T F T M S X
R X H Q N G L R W I O T J T E E W C
B S C E N E L J I J M Y L I M E B H
Y S E B G R R Y L E E S T A E O P T
D A A B F O M S D B D J O F C J O P
E M R Q C R O W E L L S W N H S N N
A G T C O D Y W R I D V N T B E D M
T W H T F I P F Z F K P R B U L O Z
H D I R U N T S A E L I I M V B C B
G D S T N A S D D T B G O G P U T B
E A N Y E R X B G D P N B E J O O P
N P P F R Y T R L Y I R G O C R R P
J P Q L A Q G I S A K N T R L T N P
S E R K L Z H K X X I C W G G K T F
J N J Y G C X Q Q D A C Q E S L K C
Y D V V M F G W D Y D V K V P V N Z
G I P L D Z B E M K S Q P S S Z W J
B X C M H J W X J B V C F P L Y T Z
```

'Choose the ___ important day of your life; it will be important enough.' (5)
'Oh, ___, you are too wonderful for anybody to realize you!' (5)
'You've got to love ___ to have ___.' (4)
Act division (5)
Author (6)
Burial ceremony (7)
Craig; Mrs. Gibbs's nephew (3)
Emily died during this (10)
Everyone has a right to their own (8)
George & Rebecca talk about it before going to sleep. (4)
Gossipy choir member (6)
Grover's ___ (7)
He delivers newspapers (7)
His drinking problem is a scandal. (7)
Marriage ceremony (7)
Milk man (7)
Mr. Gibbs died of it. (9)
Mr. Gibbs is one (6)
Mr. Webb's occupation (6)
Not unusual; routine (8)
Our ___ (4)
Play division (3)
Rebecca's brother (6)
Rebecca's last name (5)
Setting for most of Act III (8)
She married George. (5)
Stage ___ gives the audience background information (7)
The end of one's life (5)
Wally Webb's burst (8)
What the ladies did at the wedding (5)

Our Town Word Search 1 Answer Key

Words are placed backwards, forward, diagonally, up and down. Clues listed below can help you find the words. Circle the hidden vocabulary words in the maze.

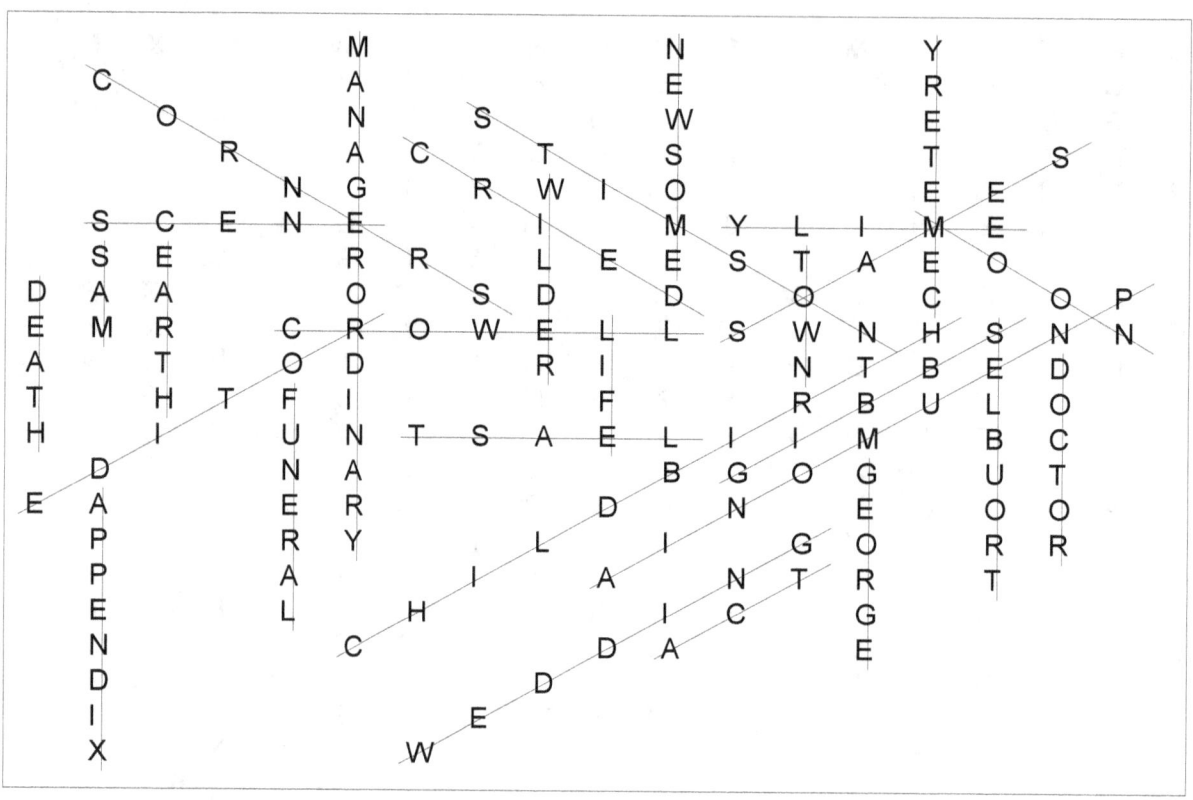

'Choose the ___ important day of your life; it will be important enough.' (5)
'Oh, ___, you are too wonderful for anybody to realize you!' (5)
'You've got to love ___ to have ___.' (4)
Act division (5)
Author (6)
Burial ceremony (7)
Craig; Mrs. Gibbs's nephew (3)
Emily died during this (10)
Everyone has a right to their own (8)
George & Rebecca talk about it before going to sleep. (4)
Gossipy choir member (6)
Grover's ___ (7)
He delivers newspapers (7)
His drinking problem is a scandal. (7)
Marriage ceremony (7)
Milk man (7)

Mr. Gibbs died of it. (9)
Mr. Gibbs is one (6)
Mr. Webb's occupation (6)
Not unusual; routine (8)
Our ___ (4)
Play division (3)
Rebecca's brother (6)
Rebecca's last name (5)
Setting for most of Act III (8)
She married George. (5)
Stage ___ gives the audience background information (7)
The end of one's life (5)
Wally Webb's burst (8)
What the ladies did at the wedding (5)

Our Town Word Search 2

Words are placed backwards, forward, diagonally, up and down. Clues listed below can help you find the words. Circle the hidden vocabulary words in the maze.

```
R L C F V B R C M Y Y Z L B L S N J
P J H G T H E F Y D R N S P C Y Y Q
K P I L J F G J Z C E X K F R V H V
P N L B K V A E J L T N M A F J W L
M E D T O W N P L L E W O R C W I S
V U B J Z E A C R F M B D R V T L V
L M I T C R M E I B E B I E R V D L
Z O R S W H L L M V C E S O A M E S
G N T J T X E L A I D E T Q W T R G
B I H R Z M A N S D L C I S S F H Y
G A A S C R S P S B O Y M M T Q E V
I E B R E J T R U D H X S B O M S Q
B J D N Y G E O Q F M K O K O O D S
B P U D M N R R E P K H N S C A N Y
S F H G R T G N I D D E W K X P X C
L S M O C T E L M H I E H R F P T R
D Q C R R W O D V Z N T N B T E L G
G M Z G L S R Q W H L F O P G N D R
R P S L Q Y G O R D I N A R Y D G N
L J W G P S E M G C Z S S B C I B X
S Z S H R J R W V W B K M V Z X Y P
```

'Choose the ___ important day of your life; it will be important enough.' (5)
'Oh, ___, you are too wonderful for anybody to realize you!' (5)
'You've got to love ___ to have ___.' (4)
Act division (5)
Author (6)
Burial ceremony (7)
Craig; Mrs. Gibbs's nephew (3)
Emily died during this (10)
Everyone has a right to their own (8)
George & Rebecca talk about it before going to sleep. (4)
Gossipy choir member (6)
Grover's ___ (7)
He delivers newspapers (7)
His drinking problem is a scandal. (7)
Marriage ceremony (7)
Milk man (7)

Mr. Gibbs died of it. (9)
Mr. Gibbs is one (6)
Mr. Webb's occupation (6)
Not unusual; routine (8)
Our ___ (4)
Play division (3)
Rebecca's brother (6)
Rebecca's last name (5)
Setting for most of Act III (8)
She married George. (5)
Stage ___ gives the audience background information (7)
The end of one's life (5)
Wally Webb's burst (8)
What the ladies did at the wedding (5)

Our Town Word Search 2 Answer Key

Words are placed backwards, forward, diagonally, up and down. Clues listed below can help you find the words. Circle the hidden vocabulary words in the maze.

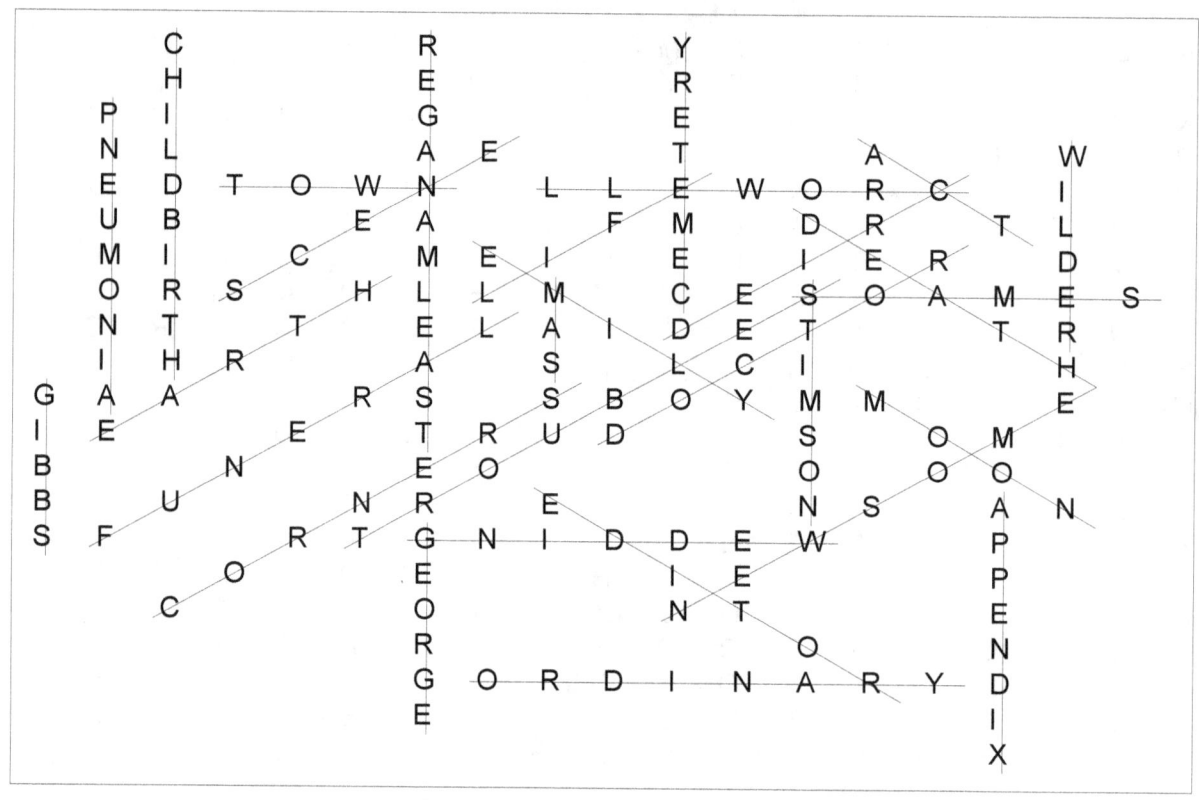

'Choose the ___ important day of your life; it will be important enough.' (5)
'Oh, ___, you are too wonderful for anybody to realize you!' (5)
'You've got to love ___ to have ___.' (4)
Act division (5)
Author (6)
Burial ceremony (7)
Craig; Mrs. Gibbs's nephew (3)
Emily died during this (10)
Everyone has a right to their own (8)
George & Rebecca talk about it before going to sleep. (4)
Gossipy choir member (6)
Grover's ___ (7)
He delivers newspapers (7)
His drinking problem is a scandal. (7)
Marriage ceremony (7)
Milk man (7)

Mr. Gibbs died of it. (9)
Mr. Gibbs is one (6)
Mr. Webb's occupation (6)
Not unusual; routine (8)
Our ___ (4)
Play division (3)
Rebecca's brother (6)
Rebecca's last name (5)
Setting for most of Act III (8)
She married George. (5)
Stage ___ gives the audience background information (7)
The end of one's life (5)
Wally Webb's burst (8)
What the ladies did at the wedding (5)

32
Copyrighted

Our Town Word Search 3

Words are placed backwards, forward, diagonally, up and down. Words listed below are included in the maze. Circle the hidden vocabulary words in the maze.

A	P	P	E	N	D	I	X	F	U	N	E	R	A	L	X	K	X
H	S	R	Q	S	M	S	F	N	W	P	D	H	B	N	P	D	R
S	L	H	F	Q	R	V	Y	Y	G	Z	P	X	R	L	M	C	M
T	Z	J	P	K	X	B	N	M	K	J	G	G	M	K	A	D	W
F	D	Z	T	N	B	S	H	R	L	M	R	R	F	W	N	X	Q
R	E	B	O	K	J	J	C	X	M	T	Y	G	I	V	A	X	L
O	A	G	V	R	W	C	C	E	Z	S	E	L	Z	C	G	Y	V
T	T	A	S	E	D	R	O	K	N	A	D	A	Q	T	E	N	G
C	H	I	L	D	B	I	R	T	H	E	S	H	R	T	R	Z	B
O	Z	N	D	I	Q	E	N	C	R	L	S	O	M	T	L	H	G
D	E	O	J	T	M	D	E	A	X	S	U	Z	A	H	H	F	K
M	C	M	H	O	C	G	R	W	R	B	Q	D	T	M	N	W	K
O	R	U	I	R	L	E	S	R	L	Y	L	I	F	E	E	V	C
O	O	E	M	L	B	O	M	E	Q	R	F	J	B	D	W	S	N
N	W	N	T	N	Y	R	S	E	S	R	S	T	D	B	S	V	F
W	E	P	K	O	X	G	Q	G	T	C	K	I	H	K	O	G	T
T	L	D	D	T	W	E	G	I	I	E	N	J	K	G	M	N	Q
V	L	C	C	J	H	N	P	B	M	G	R	Q	K	A	E	G	R
Q	P	A	K	Y	D	X	N	B	S	W	H	Y	S	L	Y	B	L
J	L	S	B	P	X	D	X	S	O	W	D	H	D	F	S	K	Z
P	N	N	F	B	R	W	T	R	N	G	D	S	T	C	D	Y	R

ACT	CROWELL	FUNERAL	MOON	SOAMES
APPENDIX	DEATH	GEORGE	NEWSOME	STIMSON
CEMETERY	DOCTOR	GIBBS	ORDINARY	TOWN
CHILDBIRTH	EARTH	LEAST	PNEUMONIA	TROUBLES
CORNERS	EDITOR	LIFE	SAM	WEDDING
CRIED	EMILY	MANAGER	SCENE	WILDER

Our Town Word Search 3 Answer Key

Words are placed backwards, forward, diagonally, up and down. Words listed below are included in the maze. Circle the hidden vocabulary words in the maze.

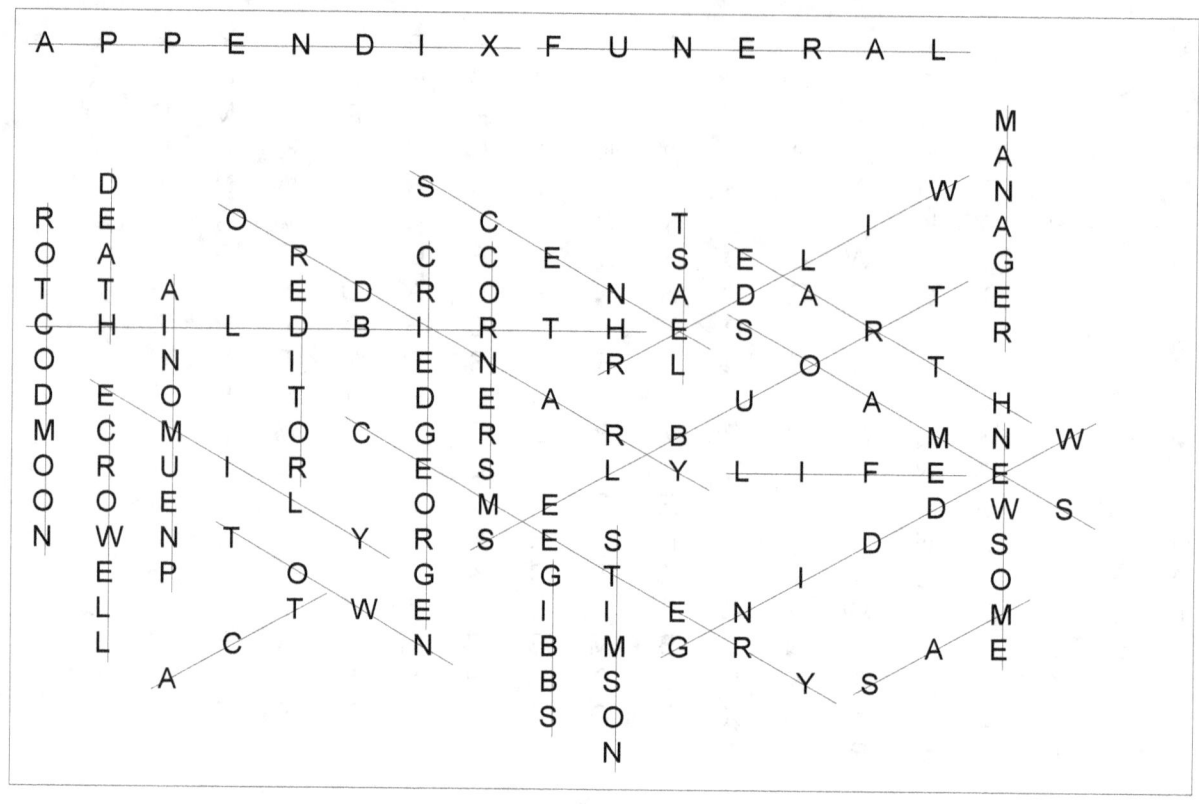

ACT	CROWELL	FUNERAL	MOON	SOAMES
APPENDIX	DEATH	GEORGE	NEWSOME	STIMSON
CEMETERY	DOCTOR	GIBBS	ORDINARY	TOWN
CHILDBIRTH	EARTH	LEAST	PNEUMONIA	TROUBLES
CORNERS	EDITOR	LIFE	SAM	WEDDING
CRIED	EMILY	MANAGER	SCENE	WILDER

Our Town Word Search 4

Words are placed backwards, forward, diagonally, up and down. Words listed below are included in the maze. Circle the hidden vocabulary words in the maze.

```
Y B V P L N Y C H I L D B I R T H G
Q V Y C N X H V X F N Q K Y T C H H
O M C P C E M X L Y Q E X G B G G K
D R D M D X U M N C J J W P N V N Y
F Y D L L L M M S Z R H D S F G D H
U R W I P Q H O O D D O L Q O Y T D
N M P B N Q E P O N F K W X F M Y R
E J G D E A T H G N I D D E W Y E L
R R S Z R Z R N S N T A N Y L D W T
A G L T T Z H Y O N M E M F L L Z S
L I H B I R V J A B C H D I G X R M
T B H M E M G N M S D Z W O I T H K
R B A Y M L S N E P S G R D C N W R
O S C R I E D O S L S Q N R R T C A
U Q X F L V X L N R C E F O J O O J
B X E Q Y W Q S E N P L T W W W Z R
L P P Q B J X N V P B I W H G N C M
E G R O E G R G A M D L E A S T Q Z
S C B M J O T J F E Z P D K M N S F
Q D R Y C C Y P J J F G H X Y J C Y
M A N A G E R C E M E T E R Y Y W K
```

ACT	CROWELL	FUNERAL	MOON	SOAMES
APPENDIX	DEATH	GEORGE	NEWSOME	STIMSON
CEMETERY	DOCTOR	GIBBS	ORDINARY	TOWN
CHILDBIRTH	EARTH	LEAST	PNEUMONIA	TROUBLES
CORNERS	EDITOR	LIFE	SAM	WEDDING
CRIED	EMILY	MANAGER	SCENE	WILDER

Our Town Word Search 4 Answer Key

Words are placed backwards, forward, diagonally, up and down. Words listed below are included in the maze. Circle the hidden vocabulary words in the maze.

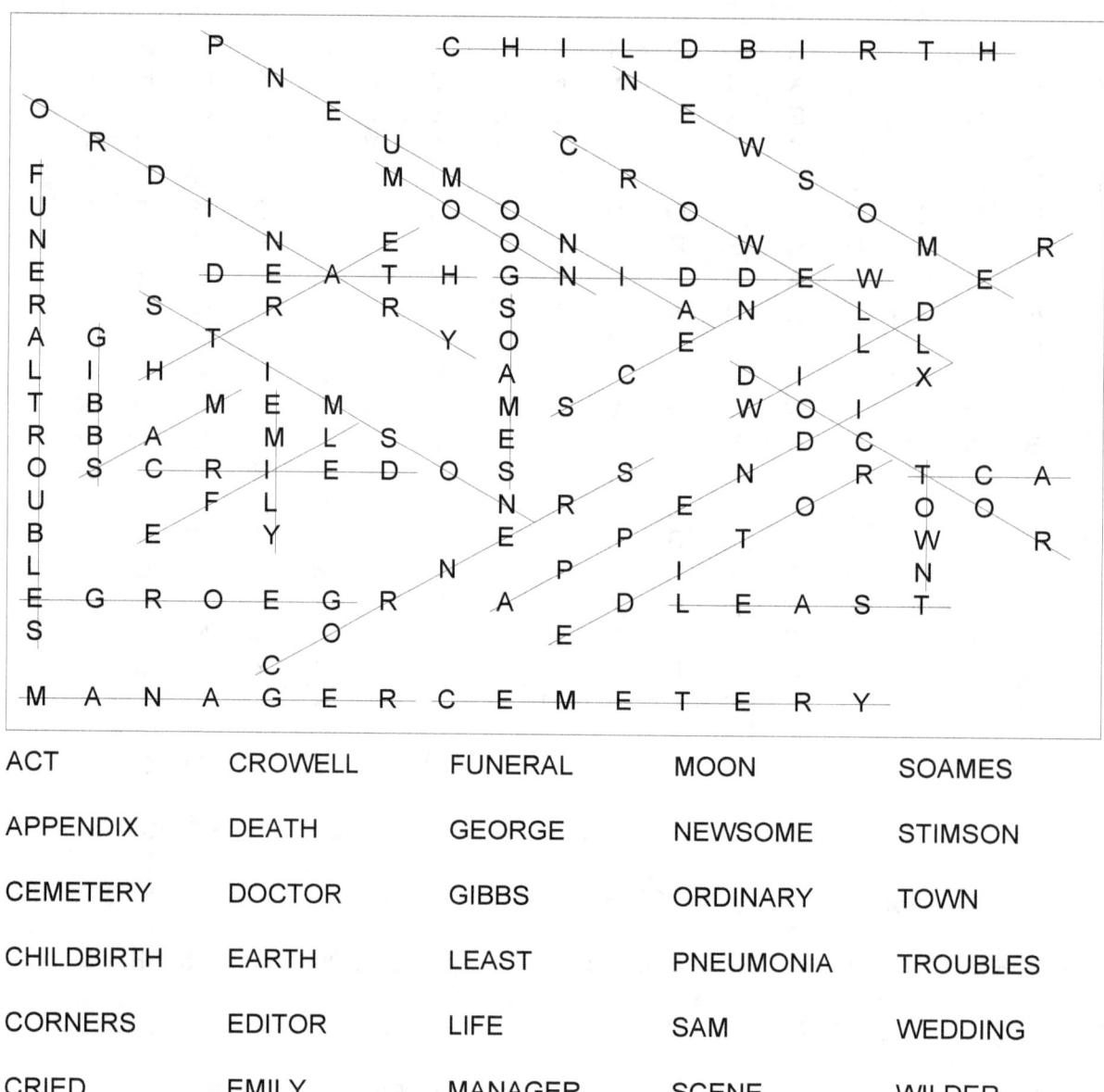

ACT	CROWELL	FUNERAL	MOON	SOAMES
APPENDIX	DEATH	GEORGE	NEWSOME	STIMSON
CEMETERY	DOCTOR	GIBBS	ORDINARY	TOWN
CHILDBIRTH	EARTH	LEAST	PNEUMONIA	TROUBLES
CORNERS	EDITOR	LIFE	SAM	WEDDING
CRIED	EMILY	MANAGER	SCENE	WILDER

Our Town Crossword 1

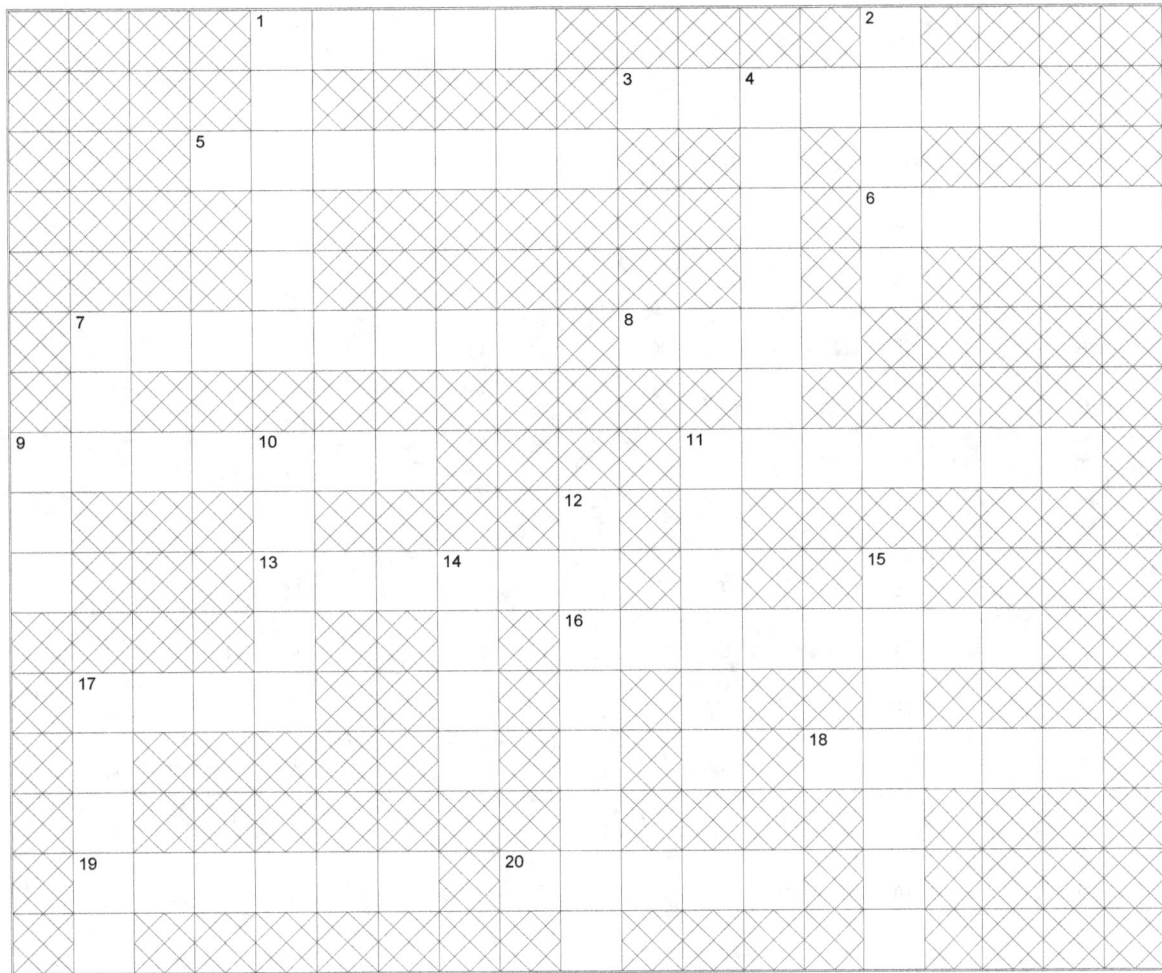

Across
1. Rebecca's last name
3. Burial ceremony
5. Grover's ___
6. She married George.
7. Wally Webb's burst
8. George & Rebecca talk about it before going to sleep.
9. His drinking problem is a scandal.
11. Marriage ceremony
13. Mr. Webb's occupation
16. Not unusual; routine
17. 'You've got to love ___ to have ___.'
18. 'Oh, ___, you are too wonderful for anybody to realize you!'
19. Gossipy choir member
20. The end of one's life

Down
1. Rebecca's brother
2. What the ladies did at the wedding
4. Milk man
7. Play division
9. Craig; Mrs. Gibbs's nephew
10. Act division
11. Author
12. Everyone has a right to their own
14. Our ___
15. Stage ___ gives the audience background information
17. 'Choose the ___ important day of your life; it will be important enough.'

Our Town Crossword 1 Answer Key

				1 G	I	B	B	S					2 C		
				E					3 F	4 U	N	E	R	A	L
			5 C	O	R	N	E	R	S		E		I		
				R							W		6 E	M	I	L	Y
				G							S		D		
		7 A	P	P	E	N	D	I	X		8 M	O	O	N	
		C											M		
9 S	T	I	10 M	S	O	N				11 W	E	D	D	I	N	G
A			C					12 T		I					
M		13 E	D	I	14 T	O	R		L		15 M			
			N		O			16 O	R	D	I	N	A	R	Y
	17 L	I	F	E		W		U		E		N			
	E				N		B		R		18 E	A	R	T	H
	A						L				G				
	19 S	O	A	M	E	S		20 D	E	A	T	H			
	T							S			E				
											R				

Across
1. Rebecca's last name
3. Burial ceremony
5. Grover's ___
6. She married George.
7. Wally Webb's burst
8. George & Rebecca talk about it before going to sleep.
9. His drinking problem is a scandal.
11. Marriage ceremony
13. Mr. Webb's occupation
16. Not unusual; routine
17. 'You've got to love ___ to have ___.'
18. 'Oh, ___, you are too wonderful for anybody to realize you!'
19. Gossipy choir member
20. The end of one's life

Down
1. Rebecca's brother
2. What the ladies did at the wedding
4. Milk man
7. Play division
9. Craig; Mrs. Gibbs's nephew
10. Act division
11. Author
12. Everyone has a right to their own
14. Our ___
15. Stage ___ gives the audience background information
17. 'Choose the ___ important day of your life; it will be important enough.'

Our Town Crossword 2

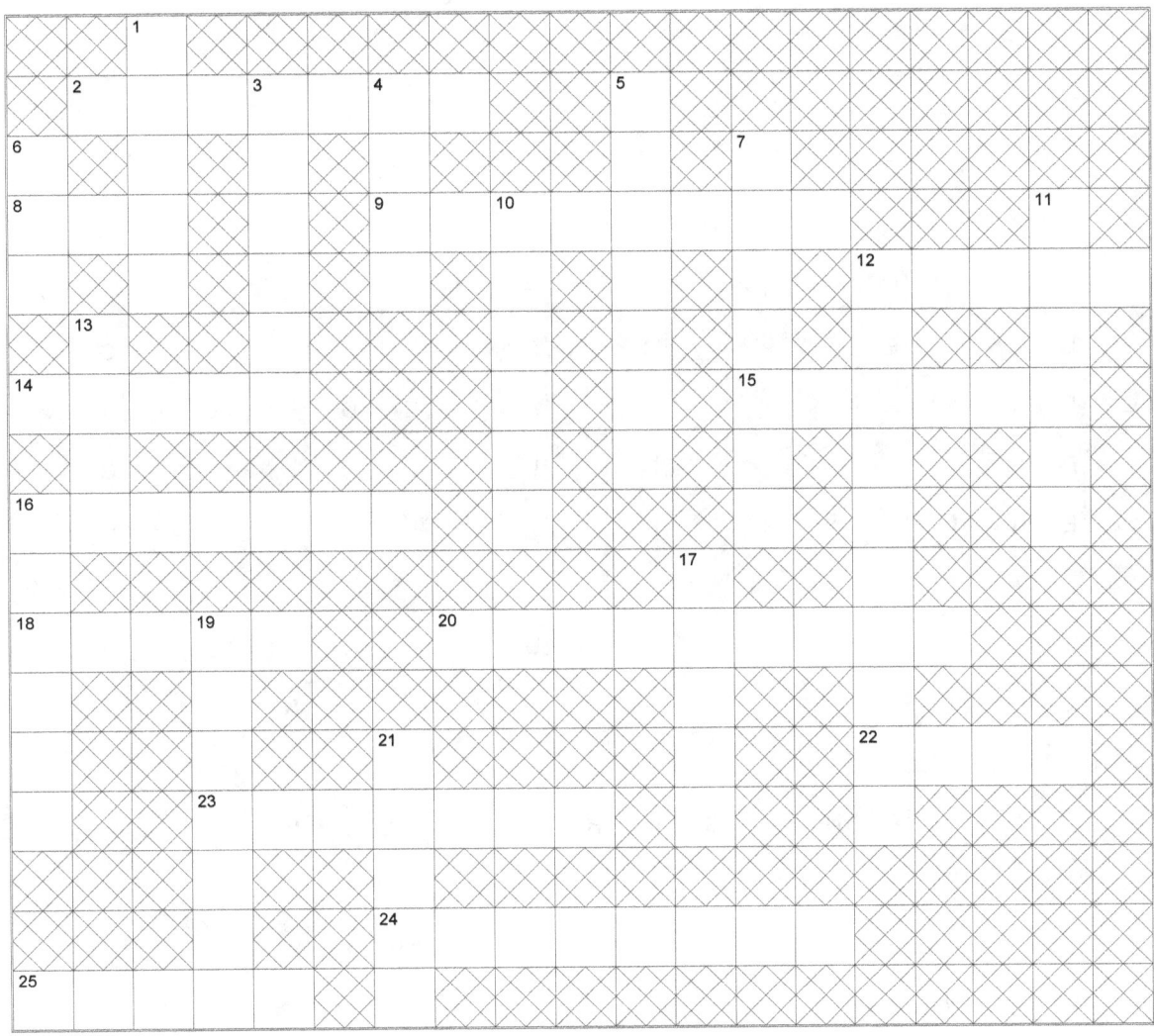

Across
2. Milk man
8. Play division
9. Not unusual; routine
12. What the ladies did at the wedding
14. Rebecca's last name
15. Mr. Webb's occupation
16. Marriage ceremony
18. 'Choose the ___ important day of your life; it will be important enough.'
20. Mr. Gibbs died of it.
22. Our ___
23. Stage ___ gives the audience background information
24. Everyone has a right to their own
25. Act division

Down
1. The end of one's life
3. Gossipy choir member
4. George & Rebecca talk about it before going to sleep.
5. Burial ceremony
6. Craig; Mrs. Gibbs's nephew
7. He delivers newspapers
10. Mr. Gibbs is one
11. Rebecca's brother
12. Emily died during this
13. 'You've got to love ___ to have ___.'
16. Author
17. She married George.
19. His drinking problem is a scandal.
21. 'Oh, ___, you are too wonderful for anybody to realize you!'

Our Town Crossword 2 Answer Key

			1 D						
	2 N	E	W	3 S	O	4 M	E		5 F
6 S		A		O		O		7 C	
8 A	C	T		A	9 O	R	10 D	I	N	A	R	Y		11 G
M		H		M		N		O		E		O	12 C	R	I	E	D
	13 L			E			C		R		W		H			O
14 G	I	B	B	S			T		A		15 E	D	I	T	O	R
	F						O		L		L		L			G
16 W	E	D	D	I	N	G		R			L		D			E
I							17 E			B		
18 L	E	A	19 S	T		20 P	N	E	U	M	O	N	I	A
D			T						I			R		
E			I		21 E				L		22 T	O	W	N
R		23 M	A	N	A	G	E	R		Y		H		
		S			R						
		O		24 T	R	O	U	B	L	E	S		
25 S	C	E	N	E	H								

Across
2. Milk man
8. Play division
9. Not unusual; routine
12. What the ladies did at the wedding
14. Rebecca's last name
15. Mr. Webb's occupation
16. Marriage ceremony
18. 'Choose the ___ important day of your life; it will be important enough.'
20. Mr. Gibbs died of it.
22. Our ___
23. Stage ___ gives the audience background information
24. Everyone has a right to their own
25. Act division

Down
1. The end of one's life
3. Gossipy choir member
4. George & Rebecca talk about it before going to sleep.
5. Burial ceremony
6. Craig; Mrs. Gibbs's nephew
7. He delivers newspapers
10. Mr. Gibbs is one
11. Rebecca's brother
12. Emily died during this
13. 'You've got to love ___ to have ___.'
16. Author
17. She married George.
19. His drinking problem is a scandal.
21. 'Oh, ___, you are too wonderful for anybody to realize you!'

Our Town Crossword 3

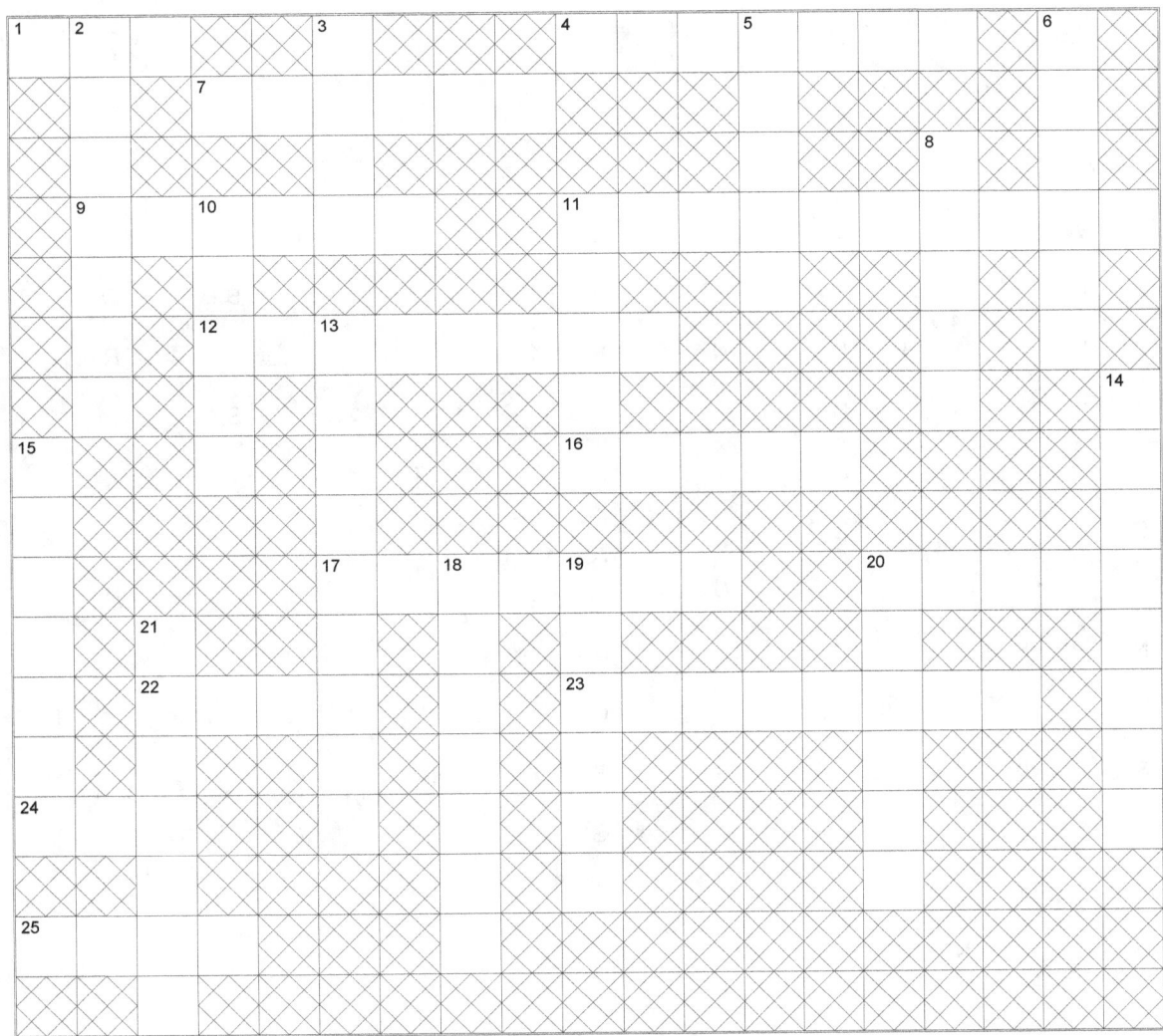

Across
1. Play division
4. Burial ceremony
7. Mr. Webb's occupation
9. Author
11. Emily died during this
12. Wally Webb's burst
16. The end of one's life
17. Stage ___ gives the audience background information
20. Act division
22. Our ___
23. Not unusual; routine
24. Craig; Mrs. Gibbs's nephew
25. George & Rebecca talk about it before going to sleep.

Down
2. He delivers newspapers
3. 'You've got to love ___ to have ___.'
5. She married George.
6. Mr. Gibbs is one
8. Rebecca's last name
10. 'Choose the ___ important day of your life; it will be important enough.'
11. What the ladies did at the wedding
13. Mr. Gibbs died of it.
14. Setting for most of Act III
15. Grover's ___
18. Milk man
19. Rebecca's brother
20. Gossipy choir member
21. His drinking problem is a scandal.

Our Town Crossword 3 Answer Key

	1 A	2 C	T			3 L			4 F	U	5 N	E	R	A	L		6 D	
		R		7 E	D	I	T	O	R		M						O	
		O				F					I			8 G			C	
		9 W	I	10 L	D	E	R		11 C	H	I	L	D	B	I	R	T	H
		E		E					R		Y			B			O	
		L		12 A	P	13 P	E	N	D	I	X			B			R	
		L		S		N			E					S			14 C
15 C				T		E			16 D	E	A	T	H				E
O						U											M
R					17 M	A	18 N	A	19 G	E	R			20 S	C	E	N	E
N			21 S				O		E					O				T
E			22 T	O	W	N		W		23 O	R	D	I	N	A	R	Y	E
R			I			I		S		R				M				R
24 S	A	M				A		O		G				E				Y
			S					M		E				S				
25 M	O	O	N					E										
			N															

Across
1. Play division
4. Burial ceremony
7. Mr. Webb's occupation
9. Author
11. Emily died during this
12. Wally Webb's burst
16. The end of one's life
17. Stage ___ gives the audience background information
20. Act division
22. Our ___
23. Not unusual; routine
24. Craig; Mrs. Gibbs's nephew
25. George & Rebecca talk about it before going to sleep.

Down
2. He delivers newspapers
3. 'You've got to love ___ to have ___.'
5. She married George.
6. Mr. Gibbs is one
8. Rebecca's last name
10. 'Choose the ___ important day of your life; it will be important enough.'
11. What the ladies did at the wedding
13. Mr. Gibbs died of it.
14. Setting for most of Act III
15. Grover's ___
18. Milk man
19. Rebecca's brother
20. Gossipy choir member
21. His drinking problem is a scandal.

Our Town Crossword 4

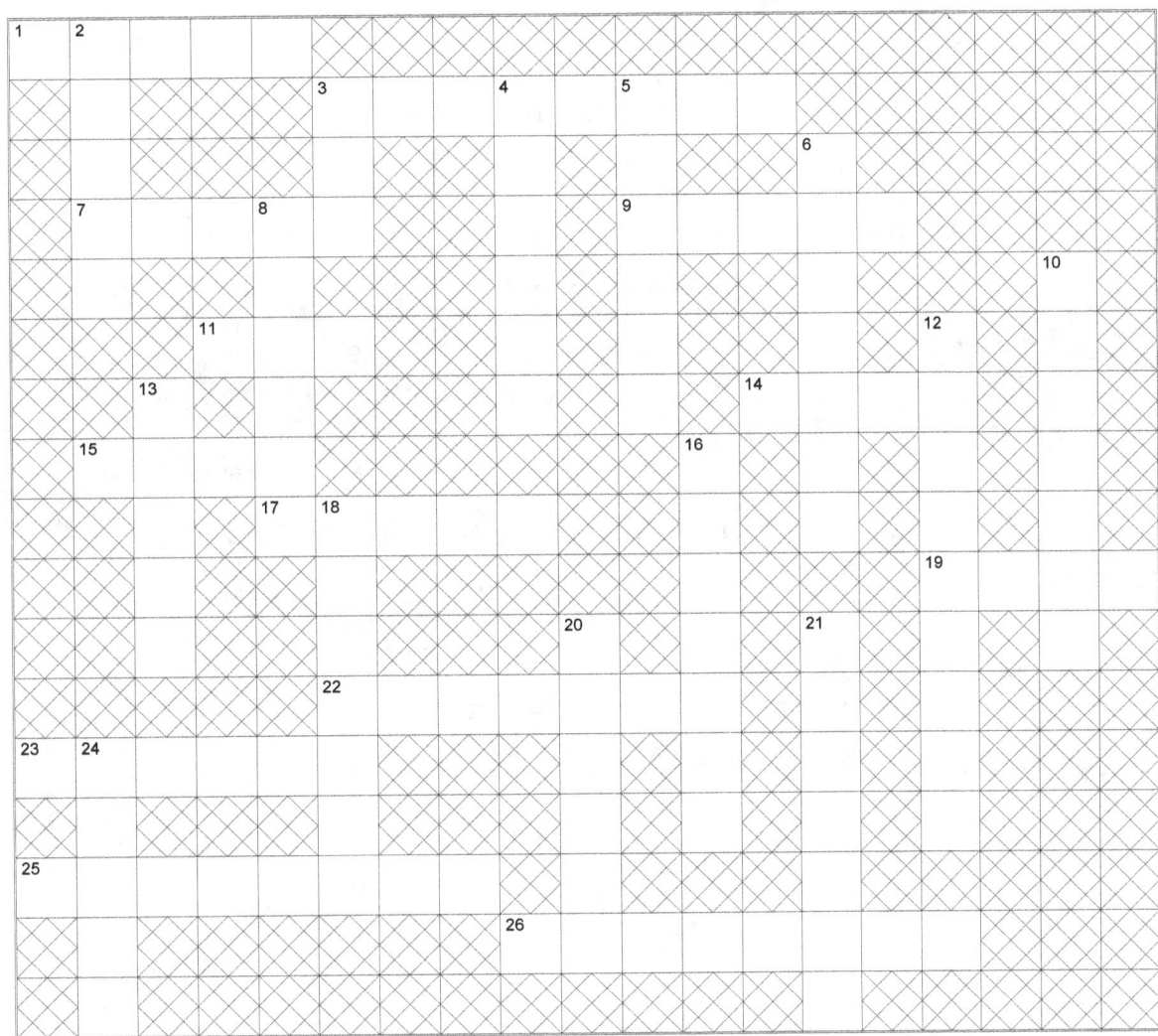

Across
1. The end of one's life
3. Wally Webb's burst
7. 'Choose the ___ important day of your life; it will be important enough.'
9. What the ladies did at the wedding
11. Craig; Mrs. Gibbs's nephew
14. Our ___
15. 'You've got to love ___ to have ___.'
17. Act division
19. George & Rebecca talk about it before going to sleep.
22. Marriage ceremony
23. Rebecca's brother
25. Everyone has a right to their own
26. Not unusual; routine

Down
2. She married George.
3. Play division
4. Mr. Webb's occupation
5. Mr. Gibbs is one
6. Milk man
8. Gossipy choir member
10. His drinking problem is a scandal.
12. Mr. Gibbs died of it.
13. Rebecca's last name
16. Stage ___ gives the audience background information
18. He delivers newspapers
20. Author
21. Burial ceremony
24. 'Oh, ___, you are too wonderful for anybody to realize you!'

Our Town Crossword 4 Answer Key

Across:
1. DEATH
3. APPENDIX
7. LEAST
9. CRIED
11. SAM
14. TOWN
15. LIFE
17. SCENE
19. MOON
22. WEDDING
23. GEORGE
25. TROUBLES
26. ORDINARY

Down:
2. EMILY
3. ACT
4. EDITOR
5. DOCTOR
6. N... (NEWSOME)
8. STIMSON
10. STWMS... (see grid)
12. PTI...
13. GIBBS
16. MANAGER
18. CROWELL
20. WAGNER
21. FUNERAL
24. EARTH

Across
1. The end of one's life
3. Wally Webb's burst
7. 'Choose the ___ important day of your life; it will be important enough.'
9. What the ladies did at the wedding
11. Craig; Mrs. Gibbs's nephew
14. Our ___
15. 'You've got to love ___ to have ___.'
17. Act division
19. George & Rebecca talk about it before going to sleep.
22. Marriage ceremony
23. Rebecca's brother
25. Everyone has a right to their own
26. Not unusual; routine

Down
2. She married George.
3. Play division
4. Mr. Webb's occupation
5. Mr. Gibbs is one
6. Milk man
8. Gossipy choir member
10. His drinking problem is a scandal.
12. Mr. Gibbs died of it.
13. Rebecca's last name
16. Stage ___ gives the audience background information
18. He delivers newspapers
20. Author
21. Burial ceremony
24. 'Oh, ___, you are too wonderful for anybody to realize you!'

Our Town

TROUBLES	NEWSOME	SOAMES	MANAGER	CORNERS
ORDINARY	DOCTOR	EDITOR	ACT	EARTH
LEAST	FUNERAL	FREE SPACE	PNEUMONIA	WEDDING
SCENE	CRIED	WILDER	SAM	GIBBS
STIMSON	EMILY	APPENDIX	GEORGE	CROWELL

Our Town

DEATH	TOWN	MOON	LIFE	CHILDBIRTH
CROWELL	GEORGE	APPENDIX	EMILY	STIMSON
GIBBS	SAM	FREE SPACE	CRIED	SCENE
WEDDING	PNEUMONIA	CEMETERY	FUNERAL	LEAST
EARTH	ACT	EDITOR	DOCTOR	ORDINARY

Our Town

EARTH	SAM	SCENE	EDITOR	DOCTOR
WILDER	APPENDIX	ACT	CROWELL	ORDINARY
WEDDING	STIMSON	FREE SPACE	TOWN	DEATH
LIFE	EMILY	PNEUMONIA	SOAMES	MOON
CORNERS	GEORGE	MANAGER	CHILDBIRTH	CRIED

Our Town

TROUBLES	CEMETERY	LEAST	FUNERAL	GIBBS
CRIED	CHILDBIRTH	MANAGER	GEORGE	CORNERS
MOON	SOAMES	FREE SPACE	EMILY	LIFE
DEATH	TOWN	NEWSOME	STIMSON	WEDDING
ORDINARY	CROWELL	ACT	APPENDIX	WILDER

Our Town

APPENDIX	SAM	NEWSOME	ACT	LEAST
DEATH	CEMETERY	EARTH	PNEUMONIA	TROUBLES
CHILDBIRTH	MOON	FREE SPACE	EDITOR	SOAMES
STIMSON	SCENE	FUNERAL	CROWELL	MANAGER
ORDINARY	WEDDING	EMILY	CORNERS	GIBBS

Our Town

LIFE	TOWN	DOCTOR	CRIED	WILDER
GIBBS	CORNERS	EMILY	WEDDING	ORDINARY
MANAGER	CROWELL	FREE SPACE	SCENE	STIMSON
SOAMES	EDITOR	GEORGE	MOON	CHILDBIRTH
TROUBLES	PNEUMONIA	EARTH	CEMETERY	DEATH

Our Town

GEORGE	EARTH	ACT	CRIED	WEDDING
TOWN	STIMSON	APPENDIX	MANAGER	MOON
CHILDBIRTH	LIFE	FREE SPACE	TROUBLES	CROWELL
GIBBS	NEWSOME	EMILY	SOAMES	PNEUMONIA
CEMETERY	CORNERS	DEATH	LEAST	ORDINARY

Our Town

FUNERAL	SCENE	DOCTOR	WILDER	EDITOR
ORDINARY	LEAST	DEATH	CORNERS	CEMETERY
PNEUMONIA	SOAMES	FREE SPACE	NEWSOME	GIBBS
CROWELL	TROUBLES	SAM	LIFE	CHILDBIRTH
MOON	MANAGER	APPENDIX	STIMSON	TOWN

Our Town

TOWN	MOON	GIBBS	MANAGER	DEATH
ORDINARY	SCENE	FUNERAL	DOCTOR	SAM
LIFE	STIMSON	FREE SPACE	CRIED	LEAST
APPENDIX	TROUBLES	EARTH	CORNERS	EMILY
WILDER	WEDDING	GEORGE	ACT	CROWELL

Our Town

SOAMES	CHILDBIRTH	NEWSOME	PNEUMONIA	CEMETERY
CROWELL	ACT	GEORGE	WEDDING	WILDER
EMILY	CORNERS	FREE SPACE	TROUBLES	APPENDIX
LEAST	CRIED	EDITOR	STIMSON	LIFE
SAM	DOCTOR	FUNERAL	SCENE	ORDINARY

Our Town

DEATH	GEORGE	TROUBLES	SCENE	CEMETERY
SOAMES	CHILDBIRTH	SAM	EMILY	FUNERAL
NEWSOME	STIMSON	FREE SPACE	DOCTOR	ORDINARY
LEAST	MOON	EDITOR	TOWN	EARTH
MANAGER	CROWELL	WILDER	LIFE	ACT

Our Town

WEDDING	CORNERS	CRIED	GIBBS	APPENDIX
ACT	LIFE	WILDER	CROWELL	MANAGER
EARTH	TOWN	FREE SPACE	MOON	LEAST
ORDINARY	DOCTOR	PNEUMONIA	STIMSON	NEWSOME
FUNERAL	EMILY	SAM	CHILDBIRTH	SOAMES

Our Town

STIMSON	EDITOR	MOON	TOWN	DEATH
CORNERS	GIBBS	MANAGER	DOCTOR	ACT
FUNERAL	WILDER	FREE SPACE	SOAMES	WEDDING
CHILDBIRTH	NEWSOME	CRIED	TROUBLES	ORDINARY
CEMETERY	PNEUMONIA	GEORGE	APPENDIX	EARTH

Our Town

LIFE	SAM	CROWELL	SCENE	LEAST
EARTH	APPENDIX	GEORGE	PNEUMONIA	CEMETERY
ORDINARY	TROUBLES	FREE SPACE	NEWSOME	CHILDBIRTH
WEDDING	SOAMES	EMILY	WILDER	FUNERAL
ACT	DOCTOR	MANAGER	GIBBS	CORNERS

Our Town

SOAMES	SAM	CEMETERY	TROUBLES	STIMSON
SCENE	CORNERS	EMILY	ACT	EARTH
ORDINARY	CHILDBIRTH	FREE SPACE	DEATH	NEWSOME
PNEUMONIA	FUNERAL	TOWN	MOON	EDITOR
LIFE	WILDER	GEORGE	CROWELL	APPENDIX

Our Town

LEAST	DOCTOR	WEDDING	CRIED	MANAGER
APPENDIX	CROWELL	GEORGE	WILDER	LIFE
EDITOR	MOON	FREE SPACE	FUNERAL	PNEUMONIA
NEWSOME	DEATH	GIBBS	CHILDBIRTH	ORDINARY
EARTH	ACT	EMILY	CORNERS	SCENE

Our Town

GIBBS	EMILY	LEAST	LIFE	SAM
GEORGE	APPENDIX	EDITOR	CHILDBIRTH	ACT
PNEUMONIA	STIMSON	FREE SPACE	SOAMES	MOON
EARTH	CRIED	SCENE	DOCTOR	FUNERAL
ORDINARY	CEMETERY	DEATH	TROUBLES	NEWSOME

Our Town

MANAGER	TOWN	WILDER	CORNERS	CROWELL
NEWSOME	TROUBLES	DEATH	CEMETERY	ORDINARY
FUNERAL	DOCTOR	FREE SPACE	CRIED	EARTH
MOON	SOAMES	WEDDING	STIMSON	PNEUMONIA
ACT	CHILDBIRTH	EDITOR	APPENDIX	GEORGE

Our Town

DOCTOR	CORNERS	ORDINARY	APPENDIX	ACT
EDITOR	DEATH	TOWN	LIFE	SCENE
CRIED	MOON	FREE SPACE	GIBBS	MANAGER
SAM	EMILY	GEORGE	SOAMES	CHILDBIRTH
FUNERAL	STIMSON	LEAST	TROUBLES	CEMETERY

Our Town

CROWELL	WEDDING	WILDER	NEWSOME	EARTH
CEMETERY	TROUBLES	LEAST	STIMSON	FUNERAL
CHILDBIRTH	SOAMES	FREE SPACE	EMILY	SAM
MANAGER	GIBBS	PNEUMONIA	MOON	CRIED
SCENE	LIFE	TOWN	DEATH	EDITOR

Our Town

ORDINARY	STIMSON	CHILDBIRTH	APPENDIX	MOON
GIBBS	GEORGE	WILDER	EARTH	CRIED
SOAMES	DEATH	FREE SPACE	NEWSOME	EDITOR
CEMETERY	SAM	EMILY	ACT	PNEUMONIA
DOCTOR	CROWELL	CORNERS	FUNERAL	LIFE

Our Town

WEDDING	LEAST	MANAGER	TROUBLES	TOWN
LIFE	FUNERAL	CORNERS	CROWELL	DOCTOR
PNEUMONIA	ACT	FREE SPACE	SAM	CEMETERY
EDITOR	NEWSOME	SCENE	DEATH	SOAMES
CRIED	EARTH	WILDER	GEORGE	GIBBS

Our Town

CEMETERY	ORDINARY	DEATH	STIMSON	EARTH
CROWELL	WILDER	GIBBS	EDITOR	CORNERS
FUNERAL	SAM	FREE SPACE	SOAMES	GEORGE
MOON	APPENDIX	TOWN	MANAGER	ACT
LIFE	NEWSOME	LEAST	PNEUMONIA	TROUBLES

Our Town

WEDDING	DOCTOR	SCENE	EMILY	CHILDBIRTH
TROUBLES	PNEUMONIA	LEAST	NEWSOME	LIFE
ACT	MANAGER	FREE SPACE	APPENDIX	MOON
GEORGE	SOAMES	CRIED	SAM	FUNERAL
CORNERS	EDITOR	GIBBS	WILDER	CROWELL

Our Town

CHILDBIRTH	GIBBS	TROUBLES	GEORGE	SCENE
MOON	CEMETERY	CROWELL	CORNERS	DEATH
FUNERAL	SAM	FREE SPACE	LIFE	ORDINARY
EMILY	TOWN	NEWSOME	STIMSON	MANAGER
PNEUMONIA	CRIED	DOCTOR	WEDDING	EARTH

Our Town

ACT	SOAMES	WILDER	LEAST	APPENDIX
EARTH	WEDDING	DOCTOR	CRIED	PNEUMONIA
MANAGER	STIMSON	FREE SPACE	TOWN	EMILY
ORDINARY	LIFE	EDITOR	SAM	FUNERAL
DEATH	CORNERS	CROWELL	CEMETERY	MOON

Our Town

GEORGE	DEATH	CEMETERY	WEDDING	EARTH
TOWN	APPENDIX	CROWELL	EMILY	STIMSON
DOCTOR	NEWSOME	FREE SPACE	LEAST	EDITOR
MANAGER	CHILDBIRTH	ORDINARY	GIBBS	LIFE
FUNERAL	SOAMES	PNEUMONIA	TROUBLES	CRIED

Our Town

MOON	ACT	SAM	CORNERS	WILDER
CRIED	TROUBLES	PNEUMONIA	SOAMES	FUNERAL
LIFE	GIBBS	FREE SPACE	CHILDBIRTH	MANAGER
EDITOR	LEAST	SCENE	NEWSOME	DOCTOR
STIMSON	EMILY	CROWELL	APPENDIX	TOWN

Our Town

MANAGER	APPENDIX	CRIED	CROWELL	EARTH
ACT	PNEUMONIA	MOON	DEATH	DOCTOR
FUNERAL	NEWSOME	FREE SPACE	TROUBLES	SOAMES
GIBBS	EDITOR	WEDDING	CEMETERY	CHILDBIRTH
SCENE	CORNERS	ORDINARY	STIMSON	LEAST

Our Town

GEORGE	SAM	TOWN	LIFE	WILDER
LEAST	STIMSON	ORDINARY	CORNERS	SCENE
CHILDBIRTH	CEMETERY	FREE SPACE	EDITOR	GIBBS
SOAMES	TROUBLES	EMILY	NEWSOME	FUNERAL
DOCTOR	DEATH	MOON	PNEUMONIA	ACT

Our Town

STIMSON	SAM	EDITOR	WEDDING	GIBBS
LEAST	GEORGE	PNEUMONIA	TOWN	MOON
CRIED	MANAGER	FREE SPACE	FUNERAL	TROUBLES
CORNERS	CEMETERY	NEWSOME	EMILY	LIFE
CHILDBIRTH	ORDINARY	DOCTOR	CROWELL	SCENE

Our Town

SOAMES	DEATH	WILDER	APPENDIX	EARTH
SCENE	CROWELL	DOCTOR	ORDINARY	CHILDBIRTH
LIFE	EMILY	FREE SPACE	CEMETERY	CORNERS
TROUBLES	FUNERAL	ACT	MANAGER	CRIED
MOON	TOWN	PNEUMONIA	GEORGE	LEAST

Our Town Vocabulary Word List

No.	Word	Clue/Definition
1.	ABRUPTLY	In a short or brusque manner
2.	AFFRONTED	Intentionally insulted
3.	ANGUISHED	Agonized; tormented
4.	BARREN	Empty; bare
5.	BEREAVED	Suffering from the loss of a loved one
6.	BITINGLY	In a nasty way intending to hurt someone
7.	BURDOCK	Prickly, weed-like plant with purple flower
8.	BURGLE	Steal
9.	CONCEITED	Vain; holding an unusually high opinion of oneself
10.	CONTRIVING	Planning with cleverness or ingenuity
11.	CRESTFALLEN	Dejected; dispirited or depressed
12.	DILIGENT	Marked by persevering, painstaking effort
13.	ETERNAL	Lasting forever
14.	EXASPERATION	Feeling of impatient anger or annoyance
15.	GOSSIPING	Spreading rumors or talk of a personal or sensational nature
16.	HELIOTROPE	Flowers native to Peru, having fragrant, purple flowers
17.	INDIFFERENT	Having no particular interest or concern for
18.	INJUSTICE	Violation of another's rights or of what is right
19.	LEGACY	Something handed down from an ancestor
20.	LUGUBRIOUSNESS	Gloominess; ridiculously dismal
21.	PHOSPHATE	Soda fountain drink with carbonated water & flavored syrup
22.	PROSCENIUM	Stage area between curtain and orchestra
23.	PROVINCES	Areas situated away from the population center
24.	SCANDAL	Incident that brings about disgrace or offends society
25.	SCOWLING	Frowning in anger or disapproval
26.	TABLEAU	Interlude during a scene when all performers freeze momentarily
27.	WEANED	Slowly detached from something one is used to having

Our Town Vocabulary Fill In The Blanks 1

_____ 1. Incident that brings about disgrace or offends society

_____ 2. Empty; bare

_____ 3. Stage area between curtain and orchestra

_____ 4. In a short or brusque manner

_____ 5. Intentionally insulted

_____ 6. Agonized; tormented

_____ 7. Frowning in anger or disapproval

_____ 8. Having no particular interest or concern for

_____ 9. Flowers native to Peru, having fragrant, purple flowers

_____ 10. Suffering from the loss of a loved one

_____ 11. Areas situated away from the population center

_____ 12. Steal

_____ 13. Prickly, weed-like plant with purple flower

_____ 14. Violation of another's rights or of what is right

_____ 15. Soda fountain drink with carbonated water & flavored syrup

_____ 16. Spreading rumors or talk of a personal or sensational nature

_____ 17. Feeling of impatient anger or annoyance

_____ 18. Slowly detached from something one is used to having

_____ 19. Something handed down from an ancestor

_____ 20. Dejected; dispirited or depressed

Our Town Vocabulary Fill In The Blanks 1 Answer Key

SCANDAL	1. Incident that brings about disgrace or offends society
BARREN	2. Empty; bare
PROSCENIUM	3. Stage area between curtain and orchestra
ABRUPTLY	4. In a short or brusque manner
AFFRONTED	5. Intentionally insulted
ANGUISHED	6. Agonized; tormented
SCOWLING	7. Frowning in anger or disapproval
INDIFFERENT	8. Having no particular interest or concern for
HELIOTROPE	9. Flowers native to Peru, having fragrant, purple flowers
BEREAVED	10. Suffering from the loss of a loved one
PROVINCES	11. Areas situated away from the population center
BURGLE	12. Steal
BURDOCK	13. Prickly, weed-like plant with purple flower
INJUSTICE	14. Violation of another's rights or of what is right
PHOSPHATE	15. Soda fountain drink with carbonated water & flavored syrup
GOSSIPING	16. Spreading rumors or talk of a personal or sensational nature
EXASPERATION	17. Feeling of impatient anger or annoyance
WEANED	18. Slowly detached from something one is used to having
LEGACY	19. Something handed down from an ancestor
CRESTFALLEN	20. Dejected; dispirited or depressed

Our Town Vocabulary Fill In The Blanks 2

_____ 1. Stage area between curtain and orchestra

_____ 2. Areas situated away from the population center

_____ 3. Having no particular interest or concern for

_____ 4. Flowers native to Peru, having fragrant, purple flowers

_____ 5. Planning with cleverness or ingenuity

_____ 6. Something handed down from an ancestor

_____ 7. Lasting forever

_____ 8. Steal

_____ 9. Marked by persevering, painstaking effort

_____ 10. Soda fountain drink with carbonated water & flavored syrup

_____ 11. Suffering from the loss of a loved one

_____ 12. Slowly detached from something one is used to having

_____ 13. Feeling of impatient anger or annoyance

_____ 14. Incident that brings about disgrace or offends society

_____ 15. Prickly, weed-like plant with purple flower

_____ 16. Vain; holding an unusually high opinion of oneself

_____ 17. In a short or brusque manner

_____ 18. Agonized; tormented

_____ 19. In a nasty way intending to hurt someone

_____ 20. Intentionally insulted

Our Town Vocabulary Fill In The Blanks 2 Answer Key

PROSCENIUM	1. Stage area between curtain and orchestra
PROVINCES	2. Areas situated away from the population center
INDIFFERENT	3. Having no particular interest or concern for
HELIOTROPE	4. Flowers native to Peru, having fragrant, purple flowers
CONTRIVING	5. Planning with cleverness or ingenuity
LEGACY	6. Something handed down from an ancestor
ETERNAL	7. Lasting forever
BURGLE	8. Steal
DILIGENT	9. Marked by persevering, painstaking effort
PHOSPHATE	10. Soda fountain drink with carbonated water & flavored syrup
BEREAVED	11. Suffering from the loss of a loved one
WEANED	12. Slowly detached from something one is used to having
EXASPERATION	13. Feeling of impatient anger or annoyance
SCANDAL	14. Incident that brings about disgrace or offends society
BURDOCK	15. Prickly, weed-like plant with purple flower
CONCEITED	16. Vain; holding an unusually high opinion of oneself
ABRUPTLY	17. In a short or brusque manner
ANGUISHED	18. Agonized; tormented
BITINGLY	19. In a nasty way intending to hurt someone
AFFRONTED	20. Intentionally insulted

Our Town Vocabulary Fill In The Blanks 3

_____ 1. Agonized; tormented

_____ 2. Violation of another's rights or of what is right

_____ 3. Interlude during a scene when all performers freeze momentarily

_____ 4. Flowers native to Peru, having fragrant, purple flowers

_____ 5. Something handed down from an ancestor

_____ 6. Slowly detached from something one is used to having

_____ 7. In a short or brusque manner

_____ 8. Intentionally insulted

_____ 9. Stage area between curtain and orchestra

_____ 10. Lasting forever

_____ 11. Dejected; dispirited or depressed

_____ 12. Planning with cleverness or ingenuity

_____ 13. Soda fountain drink with carbonated water & flavored syrup

_____ 14. In a nasty way intending to hurt someone

_____ 15. Vain; holding an unusually high opinion of oneself

_____ 16. Areas situated away from the population center

_____ 17. Gloominess; ridiculously dismal

_____ 18. Incident that brings about disgrace or offends society

_____ 19. Spreading rumors or talk of a personal or sensational nature

_____ 20. Feeling of impatient anger or annoyance

Our Town Vocabulary Fill In The Blanks 3 Answer Key

ANGUISHED	1. Agonized; tormented
INJUSTICE	2. Violation of another's rights or of what is right
TABLEAU	3. Interlude during a scene when all performers freeze momentarily
HELIOTROPE	4. Flowers native to Peru, having fragrant, purple flowers
LEGACY	5. Something handed down from an ancestor
WEANED	6. Slowly detached from something one is used to having
ABRUPTLY	7. In a short or brusque manner
AFFRONTED	8. Intentionally insulted
PROSCENIUM	9. Stage area between curtain and orchestra
ETERNAL	10. Lasting forever
CRESTFALLEN	11. Dejected; dispirited or depressed
CONTRIVING	12. Planning with cleverness or ingenuity
PHOSPHATE	13. Soda fountain drink with carbonated water & flavored syrup
BITINGLY	14. In a nasty way intending to hurt someone
CONCEITED	15. Vain; holding an unusually high opinion of oneself
PROVINCES	16. Areas situated away from the population center
LUGUBRIOUSNESS	17. Gloominess; ridiculously dismal
SCANDAL	18. Incident that brings about disgrace or offends society
GOSSIPING	19. Spreading rumors or talk of a personal or sensational nature
EXASPERATION	20. Feeling of impatient anger or annoyance

Our Town Vocabulary Fill In The Blanks 4

1. Violation of another's rights or of what is right
2. Soda fountain drink with carbonated water & flavored syrup
3. Empty; bare
4. Interlude during a scene when all performers freeze momentarily
5. Vain; holding an unusually high opinion of oneself
6. Suffering from the loss of a loved one
7. Stage area between curtain and orchestra
8. Slowly detached from something one is used to having
9. Intentionally insulted
10. Flowers native to Peru, having fragrant, purple flowers
11. Incident that brings about disgrace or offends society
12. Frowning in anger or disapproval
13. Areas situated away from the population center
14. Prickly, weed-like plant with purple flower
15. In a nasty way intending to hurt someone
16. Something handed down from an ancestor
17. In a short or brusque manner
18. Planning with cleverness or ingenuity
19. Having no particular interest or concern for
20. Lasting forever

Our Town Vocabulary Fill In The Blanks 4 Answer Key

INJUSTICE	1. Violation of another's rights or of what is right
PHOSPHATE	2. Soda fountain drink with carbonated water & flavored syrup
BARREN	3. Empty; bare
TABLEAU	4. Interlude during a scene when all performers freeze momentarily
CONCEITED	5. Vain; holding an unusually high opinion of oneself
BEREAVED	6. Suffering from the loss of a loved one
PROSCENIUM	7. Stage area between curtain and orchestra
WEANED	8. Slowly detached from something one is used to having
AFFRONTED	9. Intentionally insulted
HELIOTROPE	10. Flowers native to Peru, having fragrant, purple flowers
SCANDAL	11. Incident that brings about disgrace or offends society
SCOWLING	12. Frowning in anger or disapproval
PROVINCES	13. Areas situated away from the population center
BURDOCK	14. Prickly, weed-like plant with purple flower
BITINGLY	15. In a nasty way intending to hurt someone
LEGACY	16. Something handed down from an ancestor
ABRUPTLY	17. In a short or brusque manner
CONTRIVING	18. Planning with cleverness or ingenuity
INDIFFERENT	19. Having no particular interest or concern for
ETERNAL	20. Lasting forever

Our Town Vocabulary Matching 1

___ 1. GOSSIPING	A. Soda fountain drink with carbonated water & flavored syrup
___ 2. DILIGENT	B. Slowly detached from something one is used to having
___ 3. LUGUBRIOUSNESS	C. Violation of another's rights or of what is right
___ 4. CONTRIVING	D. Stage area between curtain and orchestra
___ 5. LEGACY	E. Vain; holding an unusually high opinion of oneself
___ 6. BARREN	F. Spreading rumors or talk of a personal or sensational nature
___ 7. HELIOTROPE	G. Prickly, weed-like plant with purple flower
___ 8. BEREAVED	H. Something handed down from an ancestor
___ 9. INJUSTICE	I. Incident that brings about disgrace or offends society
___10. ETERNAL	J. Suffering from the loss of a loved one
___11. SCOWLING	K. Areas situated away from the population center
___12. AFFRONTED	L. In a short or brusque manner
___13. EXASPERATION	M. Planning with cleverness or ingenuity
___14. BURGLE	N. Frowning in anger or disapproval
___15. ANGUISHED	O. Marked by persevering, painstaking effort
___16. BITINGLY	P. In a nasty way intending to hurt someone
___17. ABRUPTLY	Q. Lasting forever
___18. SCANDAL	R. Empty; bare
___19. PROSCENIUM	S. Steal
___20. INDIFFERENT	T. Intentionally insulted
___21. WEANED	U. Feeling of impatient anger or annoyance
___22. CONCEITED	V. Gloominess; ridiculously dismal
___23. BURDOCK	W. Agonized; tormented
___24. PHOSPHATE	X. Having no particular interest or concern for
___25. PROVINCES	Y. Flowers native to Peru, having fragrant, purple flowers

Our Town Vocabulary Matching 1 Answer Key

F - 1. GOSSIPING	A.	Soda fountain drink with carbonated water & flavored syrup
O - 2. DILIGENT	B.	Slowly detached from something one is used to having
V - 3. LUGUBRIOUSNESS	C.	Violation of another's rights or of what is right
M - 4. CONTRIVING	D.	Stage area between curtain and orchestra
H - 5. LEGACY	E.	Vain; holding an unusually high opinion of oneself
R - 6. BARREN	F.	Spreading rumors or talk of a personal or sensational nature
Y - 7. HELIOTROPE	G.	Prickly, weed-like plant with purple flower
J - 8. BEREAVED	H.	Something handed down from an ancestor
C - 9. INJUSTICE	I.	Incident that brings about disgrace or offends society
Q -10. ETERNAL	J.	Suffering from the loss of a loved one
N -11. SCOWLING	K.	Areas situated away from the population center
T -12. AFFRONTED	L.	In a short or brusque manner
U -13. EXASPERATION	M.	Planning with cleverness or ingenuity
S -14. BURGLE	N.	Frowning in anger or disapproval
W -15. ANGUISHED	O.	Marked by persevering, painstaking effort
P -16. BITINGLY	P.	In a nasty way intending to hurt someone
L -17. ABRUPTLY	Q.	Lasting forever
I -18. SCANDAL	R.	Empty; bare
D -19. PROSCENIUM	S.	Steal
X -20. INDIFFERENT	T.	Intentionally insulted
B -21. WEANED	U.	Feeling of impatient anger or annoyance
E -22. CONCEITED	V.	Gloominess; ridiculously dismal
G -23. BURDOCK	W.	Agonized; tormented
A -24. PHOSPHATE	X.	Having no particular interest or concern for
K -25. PROVINCES	Y.	Flowers native to Peru, having fragrant, purple flowers

Our Town Vocabulary Matching 2

___ 1. AFFRONTED	A.	Stage area between curtain and orchestra
___ 2. BITINGLY	B.	Vain; holding an unusually high opinion of oneself
___ 3. WEANED	C.	Incident that brings about disgrace or offends society
___ 4. PHOSPHATE	D.	Feeling of impatient anger or annoyance
___ 5. CONTRIVING	E.	Agonized; tormented
___ 6. BEREAVED	F.	In a short or brusque manner
___ 7. SCOWLING	G.	Dejected; dispirited or depressed
___ 8. PROVINCES	H.	Spreading rumors or talk of a personal or sensational nature
___ 9. GOSSIPING	I.	Interlude during a scene when all performers freeze momentarily
___10. ANGUISHED	J.	Areas situated away from the population center
___11. EXASPERATION	K.	Flowers native to Peru, having fragrant, purple flowers
___12. CRESTFALLEN	L.	Gloominess; ridiculously dismal
___13. INDIFFERENT	M.	In a nasty way intending to hurt someone
___14. ETERNAL	N.	Frowning in anger or disapproval
___15. LUGUBRIOUSNESS	O.	Planning with cleverness or ingenuity
___16. HELIOTROPE	P.	Violation of another's rights or of what is right
___17. BARREN	Q.	Suffering from the loss of a loved one
___18. TABLEAU	R.	Soda fountain drink with carbonated water & flavored syrup
___19. INJUSTICE	S.	Having no particular interest or concern for
___20. PROSCENIUM	T.	Steal
___21. DILIGENT	U.	Lasting forever
___22. ABRUPTLY	V.	Empty; bare
___23. SCANDAL	W.	Marked by persevering, painstaking effort
___24. BURGLE	X.	Slowly detached from something one is used to having
___25. CONCEITED	Y.	Intentionally insulted

Our Town Vocabulary Matching 2 Answer Key

Y - 1. AFFRONTED	A.	Stage area between curtain and orchestra
M - 2. BITINGLY	B.	Vain; holding an unusually high opinion of oneself
X - 3. WEANED	C.	Incident that brings about disgrace or offends society
R - 4. PHOSPHATE	D.	Feeling of impatient anger or annoyance
O - 5. CONTRIVING	E.	Agonized; tormented
Q - 6. BEREAVED	F.	In a short or brusque manner
N - 7. SCOWLING	G.	Dejected; dispirited or depressed
J - 8. PROVINCES	H.	Spreading rumors or talk of a personal or sensational nature
H - 9. GOSSIPING	I.	Interlude during a scene when all performers freeze momentarily
E - 10. ANGUISHED	J.	Areas situated away from the population center
D - 11. EXASPERATION	K.	Flowers native to Peru, having fragrant, purple flowers
G - 12. CRESTFALLEN	L.	Gloominess; ridiculously dismal
S - 13. INDIFFERENT	M.	In a nasty way intending to hurt someone
U - 14. ETERNAL	N.	Frowning in anger or disapproval
L - 15. LUGUBRIOUSNESS	O.	Planning with cleverness or ingenuity
K - 16. HELIOTROPE	P.	Violation of another's rights or of what is right
V - 17. BARREN	Q.	Suffering from the loss of a loved one
I - 18. TABLEAU	R.	Soda fountain drink with carbonated water & flavored syrup
P - 19. INJUSTICE	S.	Having no particular interest or concern for
A - 20. PROSCENIUM	T.	Steal
W - 21. DILIGENT	U.	Lasting forever
F - 22. ABRUPTLY	V.	Empty; bare
C - 23. SCANDAL	W.	Marked by persevering, painstaking effort
T - 24. BURGLE	X.	Slowly detached from something one is used to having
B - 25. CONCEITED	Y.	Intentionally insulted

Our Town Vocabulary Matching 3

___ 1. BEREAVED   A. Lasting forever
___ 2. WEANED   B. Areas situated away from the population center
___ 3. EXASPERATION   C. Vain; holding an unusually high opinion of oneself
___ 4. BITINGLY   D. Agonized; tormented
___ 5. ETERNAL   E. Gloominess; ridiculously dismal
___ 6. LUGUBRIOUSNESS   F. Prickly, weed-like plant with purple flower
___ 7. TABLEAU   G. Intentionally insulted
___ 8. CONCEITED   H. Feeling of impatient anger or annoyance
___ 9. ANGUISHED   I. Incident that brings about disgrace or offends society
___ 10. HELIOTROPE   J. In a nasty way intending to hurt someone
___ 11. SCOWLING   K. Stage area between curtain and orchestra
___ 12. BURDOCK   L. Soda fountain drink with carbonated water & flavored syrup
___ 13. PHOSPHATE   M. Spreading rumors or talk of a personal or sensational nature
___ 14. PROSCENIUM   N. Steal
___ 15. BARREN   O. Frowning in anger or disapproval
___ 16. ABRUPTLY   P. Flowers native to Peru, having fragrant, purple flowers
___ 17. CRESTFALLEN   Q. Slowly detached from something one is used to having
___ 18. SCANDAL   R. Violation of another's rights or of what is right
___ 19. BURGLE   S. Planning with cleverness or ingenuity
___ 20. GOSSIPING   T. Interlude during a scene when all performers freeze momentarily
___ 21. INJUSTICE   U. Suffering from the loss of a loved one
___ 22. LEGACY   V. Empty; bare
___ 23. CONTRIVING   W. Something handed down from an ancestor
___ 24. PROVINCES   X. Dejected; dispirited or depressed
___ 25. AFFRONTED   Y. In a short or brusque manner

Our Town Vocabulary Matching 3 Answer Key

U - 1.	BEREAVED	A. Lasting forever
Q - 2.	WEANED	B. Areas situated away from the population center
H - 3.	EXASPERATION	C. Vain; holding an unusually high opinion of oneself
J - 4.	BITINGLY	D. Agonized; tormented
A - 5.	ETERNAL	E. Gloominess; ridiculously dismal
E - 6.	LUGUBRIOUSNESS	F. Prickly, weed-like plant with purple flower
T - 7.	TABLEAU	G. Intentionally insulted
C - 8.	CONCEITED	H. Feeling of impatient anger or annoyance
D - 9.	ANGUISHED	I. Incident that brings about disgrace or offends society
P - 10.	HELIOTROPE	J. In a nasty way intending to hurt someone
O - 11.	SCOWLING	K. Stage area between curtain and orchestra
F - 12.	BURDOCK	L. Soda fountain drink with carbonated water & flavored syrup
L - 13.	PHOSPHATE	M. Spreading rumors or talk of a personal or sensational nature
K - 14.	PROSCENIUM	N. Steal
V - 15.	BARREN	O. Frowning in anger or disapproval
Y - 16.	ABRUPTLY	P. Flowers native to Peru, having fragrant, purple flowers
X - 17.	CRESTFALLEN	Q. Slowly detached from something one is used to having
I - 18.	SCANDAL	R. Violation of another's rights or of what is right
N - 19.	BURGLE	S. Planning with cleverness or ingenuity
M - 20.	GOSSIPING	T. Interlude during a scene when all performers freeze momentarily
R - 21.	INJUSTICE	U. Suffering from the loss of a loved one
W - 22.	LEGACY	V. Empty; bare
S - 23.	CONTRIVING	W. Something handed down from an ancestor
B - 24.	PROVINCES	X. Dejected; dispirited or depressed
G - 25.	AFFRONTED	Y. In a short or brusque manner

Our Town Vocabulary Matching 4

___ 1. CRESTFALLEN
___ 2. CONCEITED
___ 3. TABLEAU
___ 4. LEGACY
___ 5. LUGUBRIOUSNESS
___ 6. SCOWLING
___ 7. SCANDAL
___ 8. GOSSIPING
___ 9. BEREAVED
___ 10. DILIGENT
___ 11. PHOSPHATE
___ 12. WEANED
___ 13. PROVINCES
___ 14. BURDOCK
___ 15. ABRUPTLY
___ 16. EXASPERATION
___ 17. HELIOTROPE
___ 18. ETERNAL
___ 19. AFFRONTED
___ 20. CONTRIVING
___ 21. ANGUISHED
___ 22. INJUSTICE
___ 23. BURGLE
___ 24. BITINGLY
___ 25. INDIFFERENT

A. Having no particular interest or concern for
B. Incident that brings about disgrace or offends society
C. Something handed down from an ancestor
D. In a short or brusque manner
E. In a nasty way intending to hurt someone
F. Planning with cleverness or ingenuity
G. Vain; holding an unusually high opinion of oneself
H. Prickly, weed-like plant with purple flower
I. Marked by persevering, painstaking effort
J. Spreading rumors or talk of a personal or sensational nature
K. Intentionally insulted
L. Flowers native to Peru, having fragrant, purple flowers
M. Slowly detached from something one is used to having
N. Frowning in anger or disapproval
O. Dejected; dispirited or depressed
P. Suffering from the loss of a loved one
Q. Areas situated away from the population center
R. Lasting forever
S. Feeling of impatient anger or annoyance
T. Violation of another's rights or of what is right
U. Soda fountain drink with carbonated water & flavored syrup
V. Agonized; tormented
W. Steal
X. Gloominess; ridiculously dismal
Y. Interlude during a scene when all performers freeze momentarily

Our Town Vocabulary Matching 4 Answer Key

O - 1. CRESTFALLEN	A.	Having no particular interest or concern for
G - 2. CONCEITED	B.	Incident that brings about disgrace or offends society
Y - 3. TABLEAU	C.	Something handed down from an ancestor
C - 4. LEGACY	D.	In a short or brusque manner
X - 5. LUGUBRIOUSNESS	E.	In a nasty way intending to hurt someone
N - 6. SCOWLING	F.	Planning with cleverness or ingenuity
B - 7. SCANDAL	G.	Vain; holding an unusually high opinion of oneself
J - 8. GOSSIPING	H.	Prickly, weed-like plant with purple flower
P - 9. BEREAVED	I.	Marked by persevering, painstaking effort
I - 10. DILIGENT	J.	Spreading rumors or talk of a personal or sensational nature
U - 11. PHOSPHATE	K.	Intentionally insulted
M - 12. WEANED	L.	Flowers native to Peru, having fragrant, purple flowers
Q - 13. PROVINCES	M.	Slowly detached from something one is used to having
H - 14. BURDOCK	N.	Frowning in anger or disapproval
D - 15. ABRUPTLY	O.	Dejected; dispirited or depressed
S - 16. EXASPERATION	P.	Suffering from the loss of a loved one
L - 17. HELIOTROPE	Q.	Areas situated away from the population center
R - 18. ETERNAL	R.	Lasting forever
K - 19. AFFRONTED	S.	Feeling of impatient anger or annoyance
F - 20. CONTRIVING	T.	Violation of another's rights or of what is right
V - 21. ANGUISHED	U.	Soda fountain drink with carbonated water & flavored syrup
T - 22. INJUSTICE	V.	Agonized; tormented
W - 23. BURGLE	W.	Steal
E - 24. BITINGLY	X.	Gloominess; ridiculously dismal
A - 25. INDIFFERENT	Y.	Interlude during a scene when all performers freeze momentarily

Our Town Vocabulary Magic Squares 1

Match the definition with the vocabulary word. Put your answers in the magic squares below. When your answers are correct, all columns and rows will add to the same number.

A. HELIOTROPE
B. INDIFFERENT
C. CONTRIVING
D. SCANDAL
E. CONCEITED
F. BURDOCK
G. AFFRONTED
H. PHOSPHATE
I. TABLEAU
J. ETERNAL
K. LEGACY
L. GOSSIPING
M. LUGUBRIOUSNESS
N. PROVINCES
O. SCOWLING
P. ABRUPTLY

1. Soda fountain drink with carbonated water & flavored syrup
2. Gloominess; ridiculously dismal
3. Having no particular interest or concern for
4. Something handed down from an ancestor
5. Lasting forever
6. Planning with cleverness or ingenuity
7. In a short or brusque manner
8. Vain; holding an unusually high opinion of oneself
9. Frowning in anger or disapproval
10. Prickly, weed-like plant with purple flower
11. Interlude during a scene when all performers freeze momentarily
12. Incident that brings about disgrace or offends society
13. Flowers native to Peru, having fragrant, purple flowers
14. Spreading rumors or talk of a personal or sensational nature
15. Intentionally insulted
16. Areas situated away from the population center

A=	B=	C=	D=
E=	F=	G=	H=
I=	J=	K=	L=
M=	N=	O=	P=

Our Town Vocabulary Magic Squares 1 Answer Key

Match the definition with the vocabulary word. Put your answers in the magic squares below. When your answers are correct, all columns and rows will add to the same number.

A. HELIOTROPE
B. INDIFFERENT
C. CONTRIVING
D. SCANDAL
E. CONCEITED
F. BURDOCK
G. AFFRONTED
H. PHOSPHATE
I. TABLEAU
J. ETERNAL
K. LEGACY
L. GOSSIPING
M. LUGUBRIOUSNESS
N. PROVINCES
O. SCOWLING
P. ABRUPTLY

1. Soda fountain drink with carbonated water & flavored syrup
2. Gloominess; ridiculously dismal
3. Having no particular interest or concern for
4. Something handed down from an ancestor
5. Lasting forever
6. Planning with cleverness or ingenuity
7. In a short or brusque manner
8. Vain; holding an unusually high opinion of oneself
9. Frowning in anger or disapproval
10. Prickly, weed-like plant with purple flower
11. Interlude during a scene when all performers freeze momentarily
12. Incident that brings about disgrace or offends society
13. Flowers native to Peru, having fragrant, purple flowers
14. Spreading rumors or talk of a personal or sensational nature
15. Intentionally insulted
16. Areas situated away from the population center

A=13	B=3	C=6	D=12
E=8	F=10	G=15	H=1
I=11	J=5	K=4	L=14
M=2	N=16	O=9	P=7

Our Town Vocabulary Magic Squares 2

Match the definition with the vocabulary word. Put your answers in the magic squares below. When your answers are correct, all columns and rows will add to the same number.

A. ANGUISHED
B. LUGUBRIOUSNESS
C. BURDOCK
D. CRESTFALLEN
E. SCOWLING
F. BARREN
G. TABLEAU
H. PHOSPHATE
I. SCANDAL
J. WEANED
K. INJUSTICE
L. LEGACY
M. CONTRIVING
N. BURGLE
O. BITINGLY
P. CONCEITED

1. Gloominess; ridiculously dismal
2. Interlude during a scene when all performers freeze momentarily
3. Violation of another's rights or of what is right
4. Steal
5. Planning with cleverness or ingenuity
6. Something handed down from an ancestor
7. Soda fountain drink with carbonated water & flavored syrup
8. Agonized; tormented
9. Vain; holding an unusually high opinion of oneself
10. Incident that brings about disgrace or offends society
11. Frowning in anger or disapproval
12. Dejected; dispirited or depressed
13. Prickly, weed-like plant with purple flower
14. Empty; bare
15. Slowly detached from something one is used to having
16. In a nasty way intending to hurt someone

A=	B=	C=	D=
E=	F=	G=	H=
I=	J=	K=	L=
M=	N=	O=	P=

Our Town Vocabulary Magic Squares 2 Answer Key

Match the definition with the vocabulary word. Put your answers in the magic squares below. When your answers are correct, all columns and rows will add to the same number.

A. ANGUISHED
B. LUGUBRIOUSNESS
C. BURDOCK
D. CRESTFALLEN
E. SCOWLING
F. BARREN
G. TABLEAU
H. PHOSPHATE
I. SCANDAL
J. WEANED
K. INJUSTICE
L. LEGACY
M. CONTRIVING
N. BURGLE
O. BITINGLY
P. CONCEITED

1. Gloominess; ridiculously dismal
2. Interlude during a scene when all performers freeze momentarily
3. Violation of another's rights or of what is right
4. Steal
5. Planning with cleverness or ingenuity
6. Something handed down from an ancestor
7. Soda fountain drink with carbonated water & flavored syrup
8. Agonized; tormented
9. Vain; holding an unusually high opinion of oneself
10. Incident that brings about disgrace or offends society
11. Frowning in anger or disapproval
12. Dejected; dispirited or depressed
13. Prickly, weed-like plant with purple flower
14. Empty; bare
15. Slowly detached from something one is used to having
16. In a nasty way intending to hurt someone

A=8	B=1	C=13	D=12
E=11	F=14	G=2	H=7
I=10	J=15	K=3	L=6
M=5	N=4	O=16	P=9

Our Town Vocabulary Magic Squares 3

Match the definition with the vocabulary word. Put your answers in the magic squares below. When your answers are correct, all columns and rows will add to the same number.

A. ETERNAL
B. INDIFFERENT
C. BARREN
D. HELIOTROPE
E. PROSCENIUM
F. CONTRIVING
G. GOSSIPING
H. SCOWLING
I. EXASPERATION
J. LEGACY
K. SCANDAL
L. WEANED
M. DILIGENT
N. BEREAVED
O. CRESTFALLEN
P. PHOSPHATE

1. Frowning in anger or disapproval
2. Lasting forever
3. Having no particular interest or concern for
4. Spreading rumors or talk of a personal or sensational nature
5. Something handed down from an ancestor
6. Dejected; dispirited or depressed
7. Soda fountain drink with carbonated water & flavored syrup
8. Feeling of impatient anger or annoyance
9. Incident that brings about disgrace or offends society
10. Suffering from the loss of a loved one
11. Marked by persevering, painstaking effort
12. Slowly detached from something one is used to having
13. Stage area between curtain and orchestra
14. Flowers native to Peru, having fragrant, purple flowers
15. Empty; bare
16. Planning with cleverness or ingenuity

A=	B=	C=	D=
E=	F=	G=	H=
I=	J=	K=	L=
M=	N=	O=	P=

Our Town Vocabulary Magic Squares 3 Answer Key

Match the definition with the vocabulary word. Put your answers in the magic squares below. When your answers are correct, all columns and rows will add to the same number.

A. ETERNAL
B. INDIFFERENT
C. BARREN
D. HELIOTROPE
E. PROSCENIUM
F. CONTRIVING
G. GOSSIPING
H. SCOWLING
I. EXASPERATION
J. LEGACY
K. SCANDAL
L. WEANED
M. DILIGENT
N. BEREAVED
O. CRESTFALLEN
P. PHOSPHATE

1. Frowning in anger or disapproval
2. Lasting forever
3. Having no particular interest or concern for
4. Spreading rumors or talk of a personal or sensational nature
5. Something handed down from an ancestor
6. Dejected; dispirited or depressed
7. Soda fountain drink with carbonated water & flavored syrup
8. Feeling of impatient anger or annoyance
9. Incident that brings about disgrace or offends society
10. Suffering from the loss of a loved one
11. Marked by persevering, painstaking effort
12. Slowly detached from something one is used to having
13. Stage area between curtain and orchestra
14. Flowers native to Peru, having fragrant, purple flowers
15. Empty; bare
16. Planning with cleverness or ingenuity

A=2	B=3	C=15	D=14
E=13	F=16	G=4	H=1
I=8	J=5	K=9	L=12
M=11	N=10	O=6	P=7

Our Town Vocabulary Magic Squares 4

Match the definition with the vocabulary word. Put your answers in the magic squares below. When your answers are correct, all columns and rows will add to the same number.

A. SCOWLING
B. PROSCENIUM
C. PROVINCES
D. ABRUPTLY
E. PHOSPHATE
F. CONTRIVING
G. HELIOTROPE
H. SCANDAL
I. BEREAVED
J. INDIFFERENT
K. ETERNAL
L. INJUSTICE
M. BITINGLY
N. LUGUBRIOUSNESS
O. LEGACY
P. CONCEITED

1. Something handed down from an ancestor
2. In a short or brusque manner
3. Having no particular interest or concern for
4. Soda fountain drink with carbonated water & flavored syrup
5. Suffering from the loss of a loved one
6. Planning with cleverness or ingenuity
7. Vain; holding an unusually high opinion of oneself
8. Areas situated away from the population center
9. Incident that brings about disgrace or offends society
10. Lasting forever
11. Frowning in anger or disapproval
12. Gloominess; ridiculously dismal
13. Stage area between curtain and orchestra
14. In a nasty way intending to hurt someone
15. Flowers native to Peru, having fragrant, purple flowers
16. Violation of another's rights or of what is right

A=	B=	C=	D=
E=	F=	G=	H=
I=	J=	K=	L=
M=	N=	O=	P=

Our Town Vocabulary Magic Squares 4 Answer Key

Match the definition with the vocabulary word. Put your answers in the magic squares below. When your answers are correct, all columns and rows will add to the same number.

A. SCOWLING
B. PROSCENIUM
C. PROVINCES
D. ABRUPTLY
E. PHOSPHATE
F. CONTRIVING
G. HELIOTROPE
H. SCANDAL
I. BEREAVED
J. INDIFFERENT
K. ETERNAL
L. INJUSTICE
M. BITINGLY
N. LUGUBRIOUSNESS
O. LEGACY
P. CONCEITED

1. Something handed down from an ancestor
2. In a short or brusque manner
3. Having no particular interest or concern for
4. Soda fountain drink with carbonated water & flavored syrup
5. Suffering from the loss of a loved one
6. Planning with cleverness or ingenuity
7. Vain; holding an unusually high opinion of oneself
8. Areas situated away from the population center
9. Incident that brings about disgrace or offends society
10. Lasting forever
11. Frowning in anger or disapproval
12. Gloominess; ridiculously dismal
13. Stage area between curtain and orchestra
14. In a nasty way intending to hurt someone
15. Flowers native to Peru, having fragrant, purple flowers
16. Violation of another's rights or of what is right

A=11	B=13	C=8	D=2
E=4	F=6	G=15	H=9
I=5	J=3	K=10	L=16
M=14	N=12	O=1	P=7

Our Town Vocabulary Word Search 1

Words are placed backwards, forward, diagonally, up and down. Clues listed below can help you find the words. Circle the hidden vocabulary words in the maze.

A	F	F	R	O	N	T	E	D	E	N	A	E	W	U	D	N	H
G	H	L	K	A	X	L	T	P	W	P	G	Z	A	E	O	E	V
O	E	U	B	B	G	G	A	N	X	G	P	E	V	I	I	L	J
S	L	G	Q	R	P	C	H	Y	Q	C	L	A	T	C	N	L	J
S	I	U	U	Q	Z	P	J	J	B	E	A	G	O	J	A	V	
I	O	B	H	P	C	T	S	N	A	R	R	N	K	N	U	F	Q
P	T	R	S	T	H	W	O	T	E	E	R	G	L	T	S	T	H
I	R	I	K	L	Z	V	H	B	P	X	W	U	F	R	T	S	B
N	O	O	S	Y	P	F	P	S	L	X	G	I	Y	I	I	E	H
G	P	U	G	L	Z	R	A	W	H	H	M	S	X	V	C	R	R
J	E	S	D	F	I	X	O	D	Z	S	J	H	W	I	E	C	S
H	C	N	H	H	E	N	J	S	I	C	L	E	Q	N	C	P	J
P	L	E	S	B	R	D	D	K	C	L	T	D	P	G	L	C	D
R	M	S	L	K	V	K	G	I	K	E	I	H	V	M	A	O	R
O	C	S	Q	N	B	N	C	R	F	R	N	G	R	V	N	N	R
V	Y	L	G	N	I	T	I	B	T	F	Y	I	E	N	R	C	S
I	P	D	Y	L	M	T	A	S	F	C	E	Q	U	N	E	E	D
N	K	P	W	M	G	R	R	L	A	R	J	R	V	M	T	I	Z
C	Q	O	S	N	R	F	H	G	F	Y	F	D	E	C	E	T	D
E	C	N	S	E	K	R	E	T	R	G	C	D	X	N	Y	E	P
S	C	A	N	D	A	L	B	U	R	D	O	C	K	D	T	D	P

Agonized; tormented (9)
Areas situated away from the population center (9)
Dejected; dispirited or depressed (11)
Empty; bare (6)
Feeling of impatient anger or annoyance (12)
Flowers native to Peru, having fragrant, purple flowers (10)
Frowning in anger or disapproval (8)
Gloominess; ridiculously dismal (14)
Having no particular interest or concern for (11)
In a nasty way intending to hurt someone (8)
In a short or brusque manner (8)
Incident that brings about disgrace or offends society (7)
Intentionally insulted (9)
Interlude during a scene when all performers freeze momentarily (7)
Lasting forever (7)

Marked by persevering, painstaking effort (8)
Planning with cleverness or ingenuity (10)
Prickly, weed-like plant with purple flower (7)
Slowly detached from something one is used to having (6)
Soda fountain drink with carbonated water & flavored syrup (9)
Something handed down from an ancestor (6)
Spreading rumors or talk of a personal or sensational nature (9)
Stage area between curtain and orchestra (10)
Steal (6)
Suffering from the loss of a loved one (8)
Vain; holding an unusually high opinion of oneself (9)
Violation of another's rights or of what is right (9)

Our Town Vocabulary Word Search 1 Answer Key

Words are placed backwards, forward, diagonally, up and down. Clues listed below can help you find the words. Circle the hidden vocabulary words in the maze.

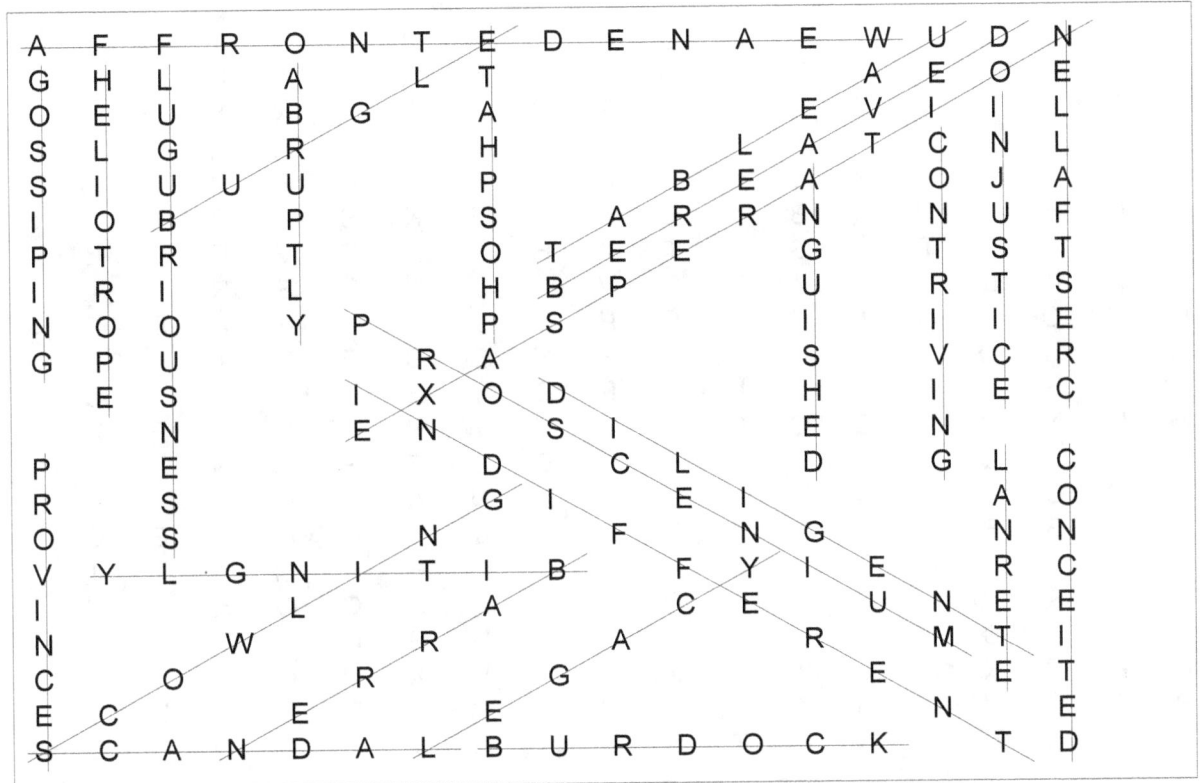

Agonized; tormented (9)
Areas situated away from the population center (9)
Dejected; dispirited or depressed (11)
Empty; bare (6)
Feeling of impatient anger or annoyance (12)
Flowers native to Peru, having fragrant, purple flowers (10)
Frowning in anger or disapproval (8)
Gloominess; ridiculously dismal (14)
Having no particular interest or concern for (11)
In a nasty way intending to hurt someone (8)
In a short or brusque manner (8)
Incident that brings about disgrace or offends society (7)
Intentionally insulted (9)
Interlude during a scene when all performers freeze momentarily (7)
Lasting forever (7)

Marked by persevering, painstaking effort (8)
Planning with cleverness or ingenuity (10)
Prickly, weed-like plant with purple flower (7)
Slowly detached from something one is used to having (6)
Soda fountain drink with carbonated water & flavored syrup (9)
Something handed down from an ancestor (6)
Spreading rumors or talk of a personal or sensational nature (9)
Stage area between curtain and orchestra (10)
Steal (6)
Suffering from the loss of a loved one (8)
Vain; holding an unusually high opinion of oneself (9)
Violation of another's rights or of what is right (9)

Our Town Vocabulary Word Search 2

Words are placed backwards, forward, diagonally, up and down. Clues listed below can help you find the words. Circle the hidden vocabulary words in the maze.

```
C P S L A Y Q E B I T I N G L Y D Q
O S L N F N L B H L A N R E T E M V
N C U F F G G T E Z N Y F Z N X M H
T O G Y R A X U L P H O S P H A T E
R W U U O B D I I G N I P I S S O G
I L B G N R B N O S Z F K S P P Q V
V I R B T U S J T X H Y L F V E I L
I N I L E P Z U R V L E P B S R N T
N G O N D T C S O F S L D V G A D D
G D U Q P L O T P H M B B P Q T I R
W I S F R Y N I E R D V E T T I F C
M L N C O D C C R W V W R J N O F H
Z I E Q S C E E T R E B E H W N E L
V G S Z C N I N N A Z N A J W L R H
C E S B E L T T N H L Q V L L J E G
V N N R N P E E A T L G E A M G N J
G T R M I L D G D B U R D O C K T C
L A D B U T L Z A H L N B H C J R X
B H G K M L W N N C A E X D F Y F B
P R O V I N C E S C Y G A B S F L M
Q N E L L A F T S E R C J U N D B Q
```

Agonized; tormented (9)
Areas situated away from the population center (9)
Dejected; dispirited or depressed (11)
Empty; bare (6)
Feeling of impatient anger or annoyance (12)
Flowers native to Peru, having fragrant, purple flowers (10)
Frowning in anger or disapproval (8)
Gloominess; ridiculously dismal (14)
Having no particular interest or concern for (11)
In a nasty way intending to hurt someone (8)
In a short or brusque manner (8)
Incident that brings about disgrace or offends society (7)
Intentionally insulted (9)
Interlude during a scene when all performers freeze momentarily (7)
Lasting forever (7)

Marked by persevering, painstaking effort (8)
Planning with cleverness or ingenuity (10)
Prickly, weed-like plant with purple flower (7)
Slowly detached from something one is used to having (6)
Soda fountain drink with carbonated water & flavored syrup (9)
Something handed down from an ancestor (6)
Spreading rumors or talk of a personal or sensational nature (9)
Stage area between curtain and orchestra (10)
Steal (6)
Suffering from the loss of a loved one (8)
Vain; holding an unusually high opinion of oneself (9)
Violation of another's rights or of what is right (9)

Our Town Vocabulary Word Search 2 Answer Key

Words are placed backwards, forward, diagonally, up and down. Clues listed below can help you find the words. Circle the hidden vocabulary words in the maze.

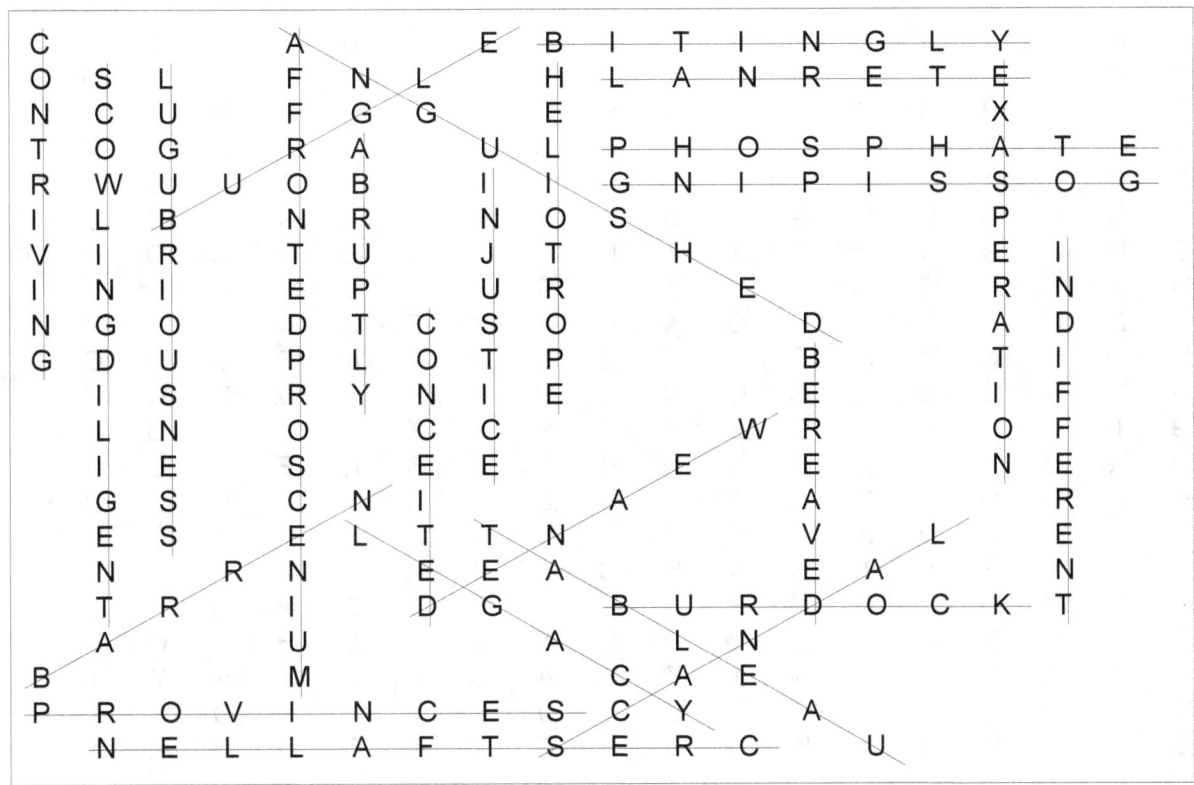

Agonized; tormented (9)
Areas situated away from the population center (9)
Dejected; dispirited or depressed (11)
Empty; bare (6)
Feeling of impatient anger or annoyance (12)
Flowers native to Peru, having fragrant, purple flowers (10)
Frowning in anger or disapproval (8)
Gloominess; ridiculously dismal (14)
Having no particular interest or concern for (11)
In a nasty way intending to hurt someone (8)
In a short or brusque manner (8)
Incident that brings about disgrace or offends society (7)
Intentionally insulted (9)
Interlude during a scene when all performers freeze momentarily (7)
Lasting forever (7)

Marked by persevering, painstaking effort (8)
Planning with cleverness or ingenuity (10)
Prickly, weed-like plant with purple flower (7)
Slowly detached from something one is used to having (6)
Soda fountain drink with carbonated water & flavored syrup (9)
Something handed down from an ancestor (6)
Spreading rumors or talk of a personal or sensational nature (9)
Stage area between curtain and orchestra (10)
Steal (6)
Suffering from the loss of a loved one (8)
Vain; holding an unusually high opinion of oneself (9)
Violation of another's rights or of what is right (9)

Our Town Vocabulary Word Search 3

Words are placed backwards, forward, diagonally, up and down. Words listed below are included in the maze. Circle the hidden vocabulary words in the maze.

```
I N D I F F E R E N T W S M P X S Q
F G O S S I P I N G W R K X Z Q S W
D J B H B D P R O S C E N I U M E P
G F W G I C G H O G C L D B B C N C
R F V Z T Y S R R V D R F U A R S L
D D K G I F G Y B C I Z X R R V U G
E P D B N Y C J J N D N T G R C O M
H P K I G G Y V J X R K C L E N I S
S C O W L I N G K H X Y Z E N K R Y
I O I H Y I D V M Z L M T N S D B C
U N N E E R G Q N T H A R E M E U V
G T J L T L D E P Z H Y X L T N G V
N R U I E K E U N P T A B L E A U G
A I S O R S R G S T L T B A F E L D
M V T T N B C O A W S Q E F X W D N
J I I R A T H A H C B Y R T X F T D
M N C O L P M B N Z Y O E S P Q C L
B G E P C G L M P D N J A E H V Q N
J J S E R V M J Z T A G V R V R Y J
N C O N C E I T E D M L E C D D P Z
B U R D O C K D Z B T X D S B G R X
```

ABRUPTLY	CONTRIVING	LUGUBRIOUSNESS
AFFRONTED	CRESTFALLEN	PHOSPHATE
ANGUISHED	DILIGENT	PROSCENIUM
BARREN	ETERNAL	PROVINCES
BEREAVED	GOSSIPING	SCANDAL
BITINGLY	HELIOTROPE	SCOWLING
BURDOCK	INDIFFERENT	TABLEAU
BURGLE	INJUSTICE	WEANED
CONCEITED	LEGACY	

Our Town Vocabulary Word Search 3 Answer Key

Words are placed backwards, forward, diagonally, up and down. Words listed below are included in the maze. Circle the hidden vocabulary words in the maze.

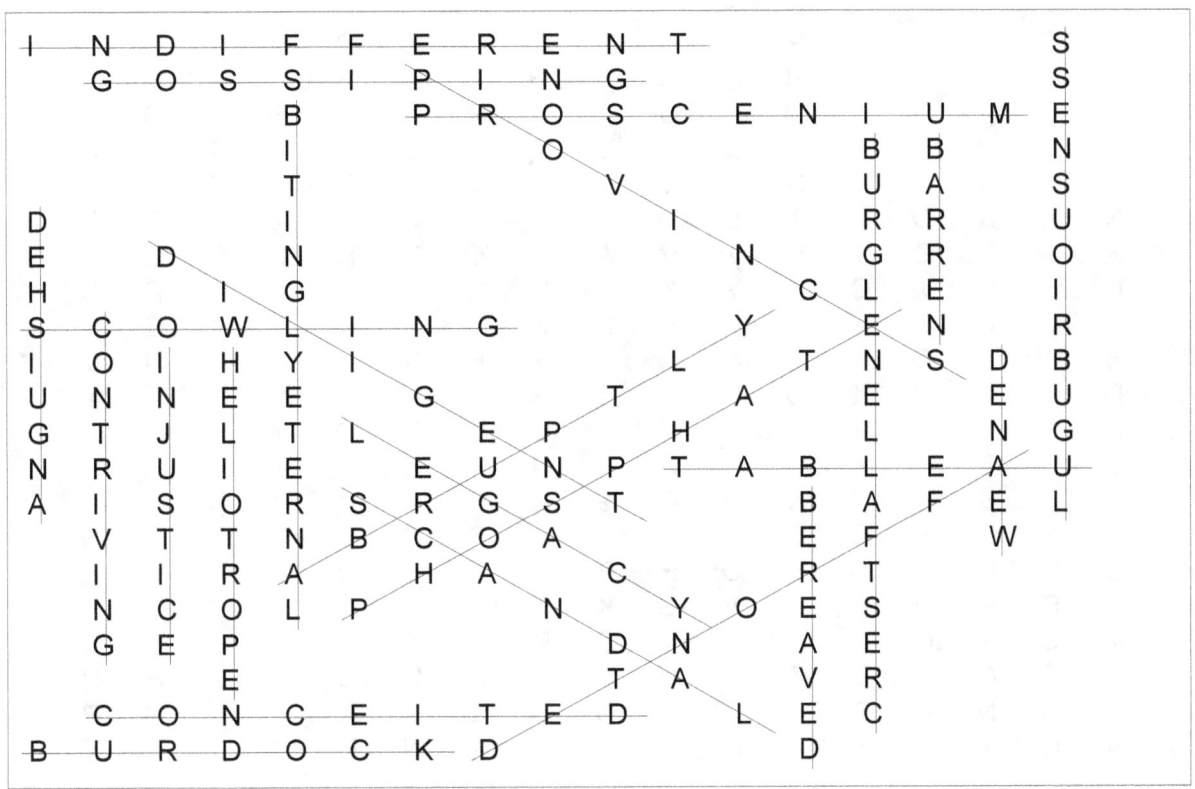

ABRUPTLY	CONTRIVING	LUGUBRIOUSNESS
AFFRONTED	CRESTFALLEN	PHOSPHATE
ANGUISHED	DILIGENT	PROSCENIUM
BARREN	ETERNAL	PROVINCES
BEREAVED	GOSSIPING	SCANDAL
BITINGLY	HELIOTROPE	SCOWLING
BURDOCK	INDIFFERENT	TABLEAU
BURGLE	INJUSTICE	WEANED
CONCEITED	LEGACY	

Our Town Vocabulary Word Search 4

Words are placed backwards, forward, diagonally, up and down. Words listed below are included in the maze. Circle the hidden vocabulary words in the maze.

```
A F S L B E R E A V E D Z R A B I L
C B C U S P H O S P H A T E F A N L
R G R G Q C M H B D D P N N F R D X
E Z K U B J A B E V W G D G R R I N
S Q P B P C S N M L V Y N D O E F Z
T N X R Q T J S D P I I O X N N F D
F K J I Z J L J R A P O I H T C E S
A K E O J C R Y X I L L T J E G R D
L L C U C V T F S F X P A R D Y E R
L S I S O K Z S N B R H R W O N N J
E D T N N X O X H O B X E G N P T T
N P S E C G H Z V G U D P Q R F E C
S L U S E N H I Z D R B S P V G O F
P F J S I Y N D E S G F A B S N D T
J M N R T C G H C L L P X U T T I N
M U I N E C S O R P E T E R N A L G
P X B S D I W M G K J G I D T B I F
L W C N U L H H M D P V A O F L G D
S H F G I D Z P W Z I J H C B E E B
R W N N V B I T I N G L Y K Y A N P
Z A G J V T F M G W E A N E D U T T
```

ABRUPTLY	CONTRIVING	LEGACY
AFFRONTED	CRESTFALLEN	LUGUBRIOUSNESS
ANGUISHED	DILIGENT	PHOSPHATE
BARREN	ETERNAL	PROSCENIUM
BEREAVED	EXASPERATION	PROVINCES
BITINGLY	GOSSIPING	SCANDAL
BURDOCK	HELIOTROPE	SCOWLING
BURGLE	INDIFFERENT	TABLEAU
CONCEITED	INJUSTICE	WEANED

Our Town Vocabulary Word Search 4 Answer Key

Words are placed backwards, forward, diagonally, up and down. Words listed below are included in the maze. Circle the hidden vocabulary words in the maze.

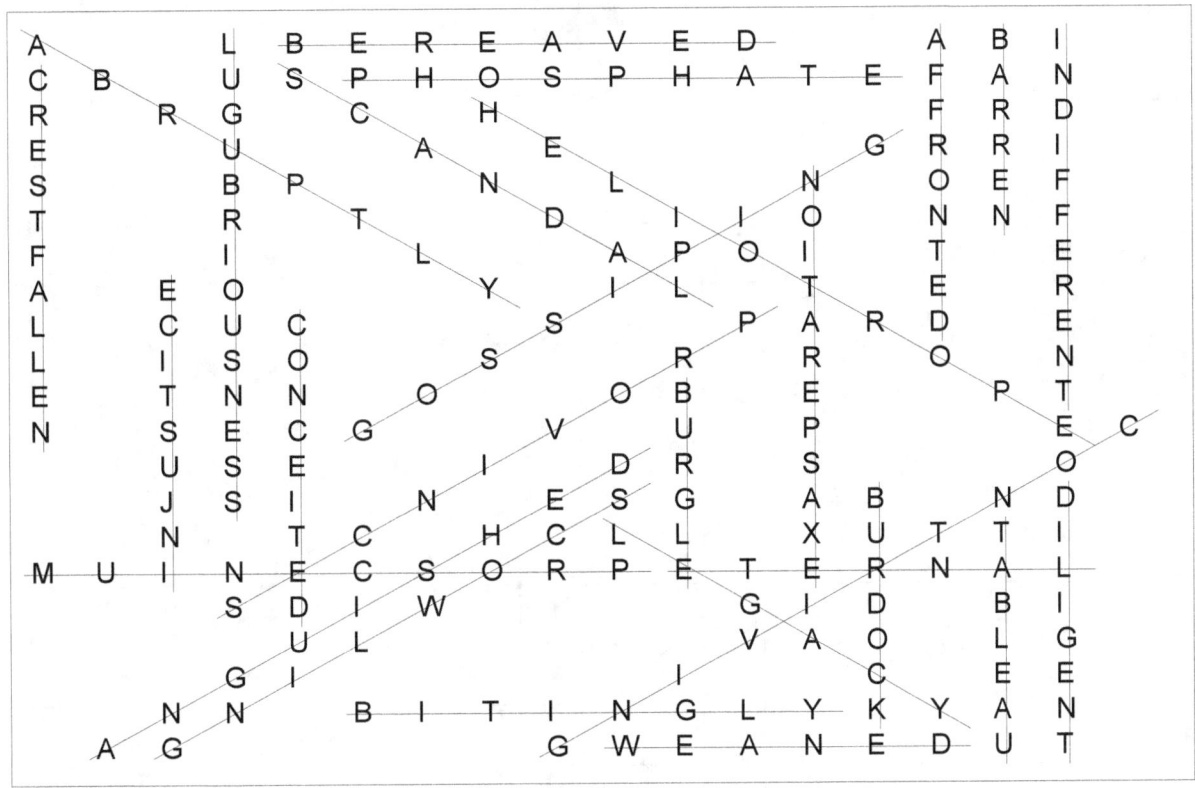

ABRUPTLY	CONTRIVING	LEGACY
AFFRONTED	CRESTFALLEN	LUGUBRIOUSNESS
ANGUISHED	DILIGENT	PHOSPHATE
BARREN	ETERNAL	PROSCENIUM
BEREAVED	EXASPERATION	PROVINCES
BITINGLY	GOSSIPING	SCANDAL
BURDOCK	HELIOTROPE	SCOWLING
BURGLE	INDIFFERENT	TABLEAU
CONCEITED	INJUSTICE	WEANED

Our Town Vocabulary Crossword 1

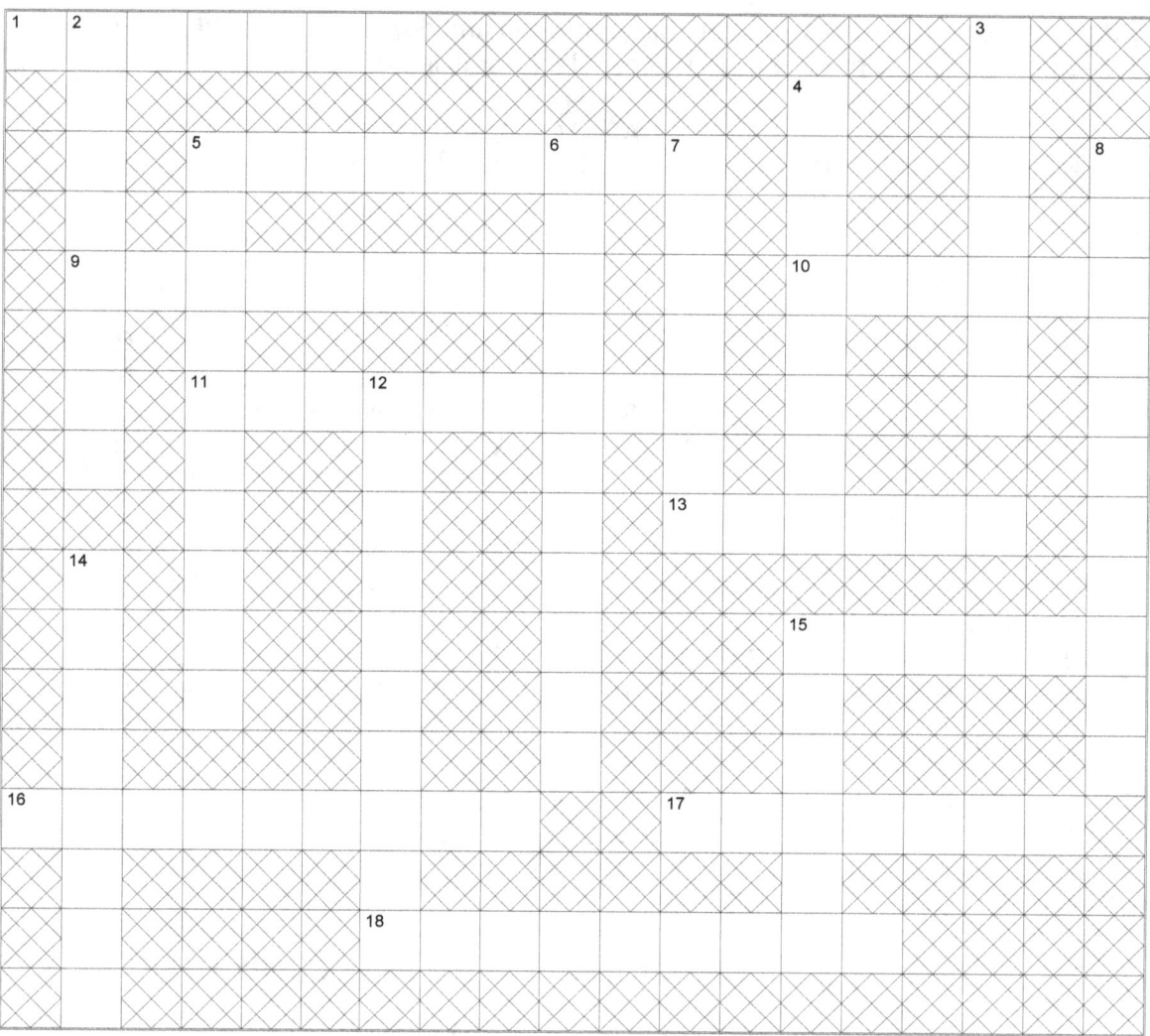

Across
1. Interlude during a scene when all performers freeze momentarily
5. Areas situated away from the population center
9. Soda fountain drink with carbonated water & flavored syrup
10. Slowly detached from something one is used to having
11. Vain; holding an unusually high opinion of oneself
13. Something handed down from an ancestor
15. Steal
16. Violation of another's rights or of what is right
17. Prickly, weed-like plant with purple flower
18. Spreading rumors or talk of a personal or sensational nature

Down
2. In a short or brusque manner
3. Lasting forever
4. Frowning in anger or disapproval
5. Stage area between curtain and orchestra
6. Dejected; dispirited or depressed
7. Incident that brings about disgrace or offends society
8. Having no particular interest or concern for
12. Planning with cleverness or ingenuity
14. In a nasty way intending to hurt someone
15. Empty; bare

Our Town Vocabulary Crossword 1 Answer Key

	1 T	2 A	B	L	E	A	U							3 E	
		B								4 S		T			
		R	5 P	R	O	V	I	6 N	C	E	7 S		C		E	8 I
		U	R					R			C		O		R	N
		9 P	H	O	S	P	H	A	T	E		A		10 W	E	A	N	E	D
		T	S					S			A		N		L		A		I
		L	11 C	O	N	12 C	E	I	T	E	D		I			L		F
		Y	E			O			F			A		N					F
			N			N			A		13 L	E	G	A	C	Y		E
		14 B	I			T			L							R
		I	U			R			L				15 B	U	R	G	L	E
		T	M			I			E				A			N
		I				V			N				R			T
		16 I	N	J	U	S	T	I	C	E		17 B	U	R	D	O	C	K
		G				N						E
		L				18 G	O	S	S	I	P	I	N	G
		Y

Across
1. Interlude during a scene when all performers freeze momentarily
5. Areas situated away from the population center
9. Soda fountain drink with carbonated water & flavored syrup
10. Slowly detached from something one is used to having
11. Vain; holding an unusually high opinion of oneself
13. Something handed down from an ancestor
15. Steal
16. Violation of another's rights or of what is right
17. Prickly, weed-like plant with purple flower
18. Spreading rumors or talk of a personal or sensational nature

Down
2. In a short or brusque manner
3. Lasting forever
4. Frowning in anger or disapproval
5. Stage area between curtain and orchestra
6. Dejected; dispirited or depressed
7. Incident that brings about disgrace or offends society
8. Having no particular interest or concern for
12. Planning with cleverness or ingenuity
14. In a nasty way intending to hurt someone
15. Empty; bare

Our Town Vocabulary Crossword 2

Across
2. Frowning in anger or disapproval
4. Incident that brings about disgrace or offends society
9. Empty; bare
10. Spreading rumors or talk of a personal or sensational nature
11. Agonized; tormented
13. Intentionally insulted
14. Something handed down from an ancestor
15. Steal
17. Suffering from the loss of a loved one
18. Soda fountain drink with carbonated water & flavored syrup

Down
1. Interlude during a scene when all performers freeze momentarily
3. Dejected; dispirited or depressed
5. Vain; holding an unusually high opinion of oneself
6. Gloominess; ridiculously dismal
7. Stage area between curtain and orchestra
8. Marked by persevering, painstaking effort
11. In a short or brusque manner
12. Flowers native to Peru, having fragrant, purple flowers
15. Prickly, weed-like plant with purple flower
16. Slowly detached from something one is used to having

Our Town Vocabulary Crossword 2 Answer Key

	1 T		2 S	3 C	O	W	L	I	N	G		4 S	5 C	A	N	D	A	6 L
	A		7 P		R				8 D			O					U
9 B	A	R	R	E	N		10 G	O	S	S	I	P	I	N	G			G
L			O		S				L				C					U
E			S		T		11 A	N	G	U	I	S	H	E	D			B
A			C		F		B				G			I		12 H		R
U			E		13 A	F	F	R	O	N	T	E	D		T		E		I
			N		L		U				N			E		L		O
			I		L		P				T			D		I		U
			U		E		T									O		S
			M		N		14 L	E	G	A	C	Y				T		N
					Y									15 B	U	R	G	L	E
										16 W				U		O		S
										E				R		P		S
							17 B	E	R	E	A	V	E	D		E	
										N				O			
					18 P	H	O	S	P	H	A	T	E			C	
										E						K	

Across
- 2. Frowning in anger or disapproval
- 4. Incident that brings about disgrace or offends society
- 9. Empty; bare
- 10. Spreading rumors or talk of a personal or sensational nature
- 11. Agonized; tormented
- 13. Intentionally insulted
- 14. Something handed down from an ancestor
- 15. Steal
- 17. Suffering from the loss of a loved one
- 18. Soda fountain drink with carbonated water & flavored syrup

Down
- 1. Interlude during a scene when all performers freeze momentarily
- 3. Dejected; dispirited or depressed
- 5. Vain; holding an unusually high opinion of oneself
- 6. Gloominess; ridiculously dismal
- 7. Stage area between curtain and orchestra
- 8. Marked by persevering, painstaking effort
- 11. In a short or brusque manner
- 12. Flowers native to Peru, having fragrant, purple flowers
- 15. Prickly, weed-like plant with purple flower
- 16. Slowly detached from something one is used to having

Our Town Vocabulary Crossword 3

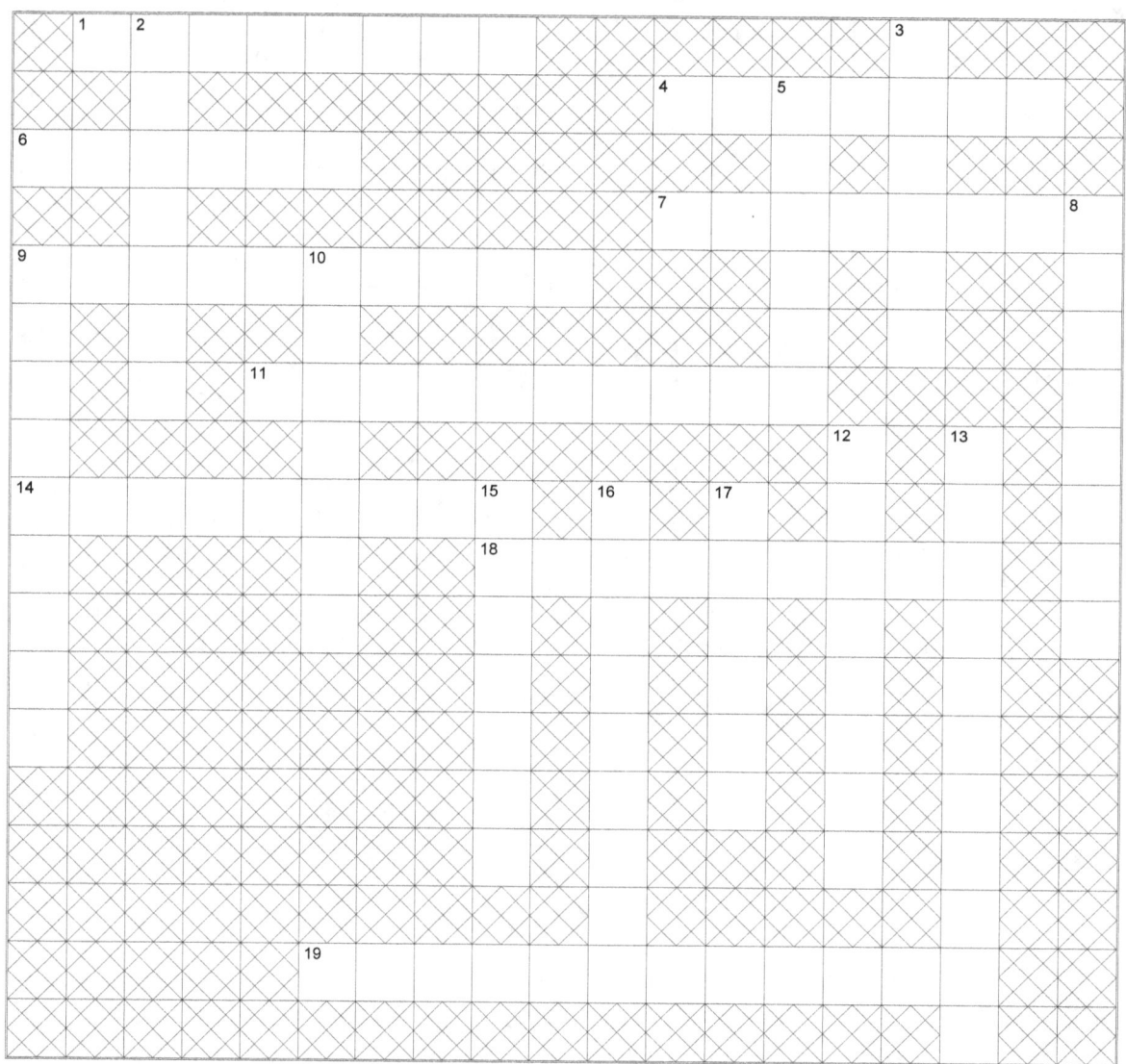

Across
1. In a short or brusque manner
4. Interlude during a scene when all performers freeze momentarily
6. Empty; bare
7. Suffering from the loss of a loved one
9. Stage area between curtain and orchestra
11. Flowers native to Peru, having fragrant, purple flowers
14. Areas situated away from the population center
18. Vain; holding an unusually high opinion of oneself
19. Feeling of impatient anger or annoyance

Down
2. Prickly, weed-like plant with purple flower
3. Something handed down from an ancestor
5. Steal
8. Marked by persevering, painstaking effort
9. Soda fountain drink with carbonated water & flavored syrup
10. Lasting forever
12. In a nasty way intending to hurt someone
13. Having no particular interest or concern for
15. Incident that brings about disgrace or offends society
16. Violation of another's rights or of what is right
17. Slowly detached from something one is used to having

Our Town Vocabulary Crossword 3 Answer Key

Across
1. In a short or brusque manner
4. Interlude during a scene when all performers freeze momentarily
6. Empty; bare
7. Suffering from the loss of a loved one
9. Stage area between curtain and orchestra
11. Flowers native to Peru, having fragrant, purple flowers
14. Areas situated away from the population center
18. Vain; holding an unusually high opinion of oneself
19. Feeling of impatient anger or annoyance

Down
2. Prickly, weed-like plant with purple flower
3. Something handed down from an ancestor
5. Steal
8. Marked by persevering, painstaking effort
9. Soda fountain drink with carbonated water & flavored syrup
10. Lasting forever
12. In a nasty way intending to hurt someone
13. Having no particular interest or concern for
15. Incident that brings about disgrace or offends society
16. Violation of another's rights or of what is right
17. Slowly detached from something one is used to having

Our Town Vocabulary Crossword 4

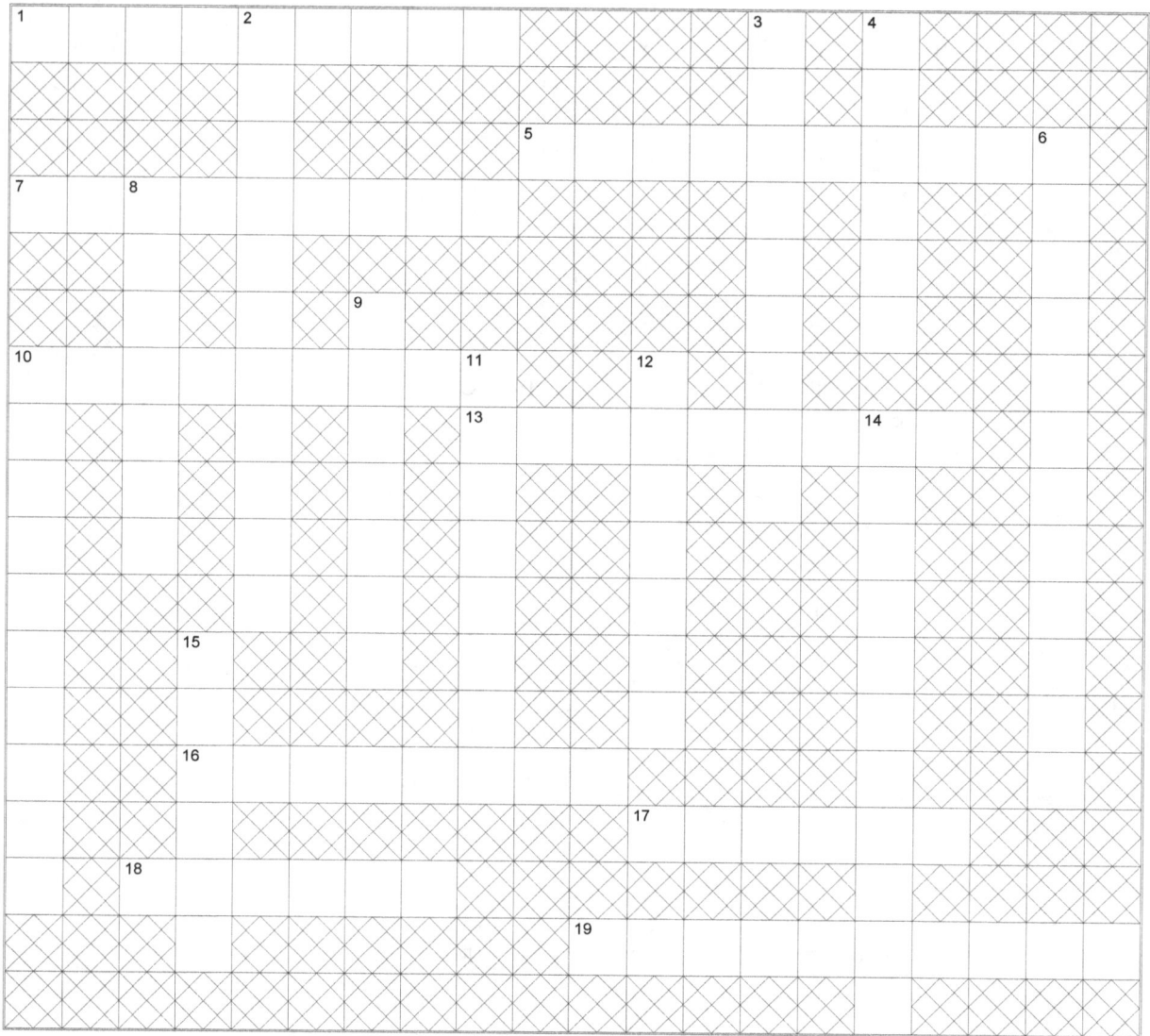

Across
1. Areas situated away from the population center
5. Flowers native to Peru, having fragrant, purple flowers
7. Spreading rumors or talk of a personal or sensational nature
10. Vain; holding an unusually high opinion of oneself
13. Violation of another's rights or of what is right
16. In a short or brusque manner
17. Steal
18. Something handed down from an ancestor
19. Stage area between curtain and orchestra

Down
2. Having no particular interest or concern for
3. Soda fountain drink with carbonated water & flavored syrup
4. Empty; bare
6. Feeling of impatient anger or annoyance
8. Incident that brings about disgrace or offends society
9. Lasting forever
10. Planning with cleverness or ingenuity
11. Marked by persevering, painstaking effort
12. Prickly, weed-like plant with purple flower
14. Dejected; dispirited or depressed
15. Slowly detached from something one is used to having

Our Town Vocabulary Crossword 4 Answer Key

	1 P	R	O	2 V	I	N	C	E	S			3 P		4 B		
				N								H		A		
				D				5 H	E	L	I	O	T	R	O	P	E
7 G	O	8 S	S	I	P	I	N	G				S		R			6 E
		C		F								P		E			X
		A		F		9 E						H		N			A
10 C	O	N	C	E	I	T	E	D		11 D		12 B		A			S
O		D		R		E		13 I	N	J	U	S	T	I	14 C	E	P
N		A		E		R		L				U		C			E
T		L		N		N		I				R		E			R
R				T		A		G				D		E			A
I		15 W				L		E				O		S			T
V		E						N				C		T			I
I		16 A	B	R	U	P	T	L	Y			K		F			O
N		N										17 B	U	R	G	L	E
G		18 L	E	G	A	C	Y							L			
		D						19 P	R	O	S	C	E	N	I	U	M
														N			

Across
1. Areas situated away from the population center
5. Flowers native to Peru, having fragrant, purple flowers
7. Spreading rumors or talk of a personal or sensational nature
10. Vain; holding an unusually high opinion of oneself
13. Violation of another's rights or of what is right
16. In a short or brusque manner
17. Steal
18. Something handed down from an ancestor
19. Stage area between curtain and orchestra

Down
2. Having no particular interest or concern for
3. Soda fountain drink with carbonated water & flavored syrup
4. Empty; bare
6. Feeling of impatient anger or annoyance
8. Incident that brings about disgrace or offends society
9. Lasting forever
10. Planning with cleverness or ingenuity
11. Marked by persevering, painstaking effort
12. Prickly, weed-like plant with purple flower
14. Dejected; dispirited or depressed
15. Slowly detached from something one is used to having

Our Town Vocabulary Juggle Letters 1

1. CLYAGE = 1. _____
Something handed down from an ancestor

2. NEWDAE = 2. _____
Slowly detached from something one is used to having

3. DLANASC = 3. _____
Incident that brings about disgrace or offends society

4. CKORDUB = 4. _____
Prickly, weed-like plant with purple flower

5. BARNRE = 5. _____
Empty; bare

6. OCNIMRSPEU = 6. _____
Stage area between curtain and orchestra

7. NPRSCVIOE = 7. _____
Areas situated away from the population center

8. FTDRFEAON = 8. _____
Intentionally insulted

9. ELNRTEA = 9. _____
Lasting forever

10. YUBRPALT = 10. _____
In a short or brusque manner

11. LAFNCSLREET = 11. _____
Dejected; dispirited or depressed

12. AREXESOPATIN = 12. _____
Feeling of impatient anger or annoyance

13. GBITILYN = 13. _____
In a nasty way intending to hurt someone

14. AUAELTB = 14. _____
Interlude during a scene when all performers freeze momentarily

15. ICNOLSWG = 15. _____
Frowning in anger or disapproval

Our Town Vocabulary Juggle Letters 1 Answer Key

1. CLYAGE = 1. LEGACY
   Something handed down from an ancestor

2. NEWDAE = 2. WEANED
   Slowly detached from something one is used to having

3. DLANASC = 3. SCANDAL
   Incident that brings about disgrace or offends society

4. CKORDUB = 4. BURDOCK
   Prickly, weed-like plant with purple flower

5. BARNRE = 5. BARREN
   Empty; bare

6. OCNIMRSPEU = 6. PROSCENIUM
   Stage area between curtain and orchestra

7. NPRSCVIOE = 7. PROVINCES
   Areas situated away from the population center

8. FTDRFEAON = 8. AFFRONTED
   Intentionally insulted

9. ELNRTEA = 9. ETERNAL
   Lasting forever

10. YUBRPALT = 10. ABRUPTLY
    In a short or brusque manner

11. LAFNCSLREET = 11. CRESTFALLEN
    Dejected; dispirited or depressed

12. AREXESOPATIN = 12. EXASPERATION
    Feeling of impatient anger or annoyance

13. GBITILYN = 13. BITINGLY
    In a nasty way intending to hurt someone

14. AUAELTB = 14. TABLEAU
    Interlude during a scene when all performers freeze momentarily

15. ICNOLSWG = 15. SCOWLING
    Frowning in anger or disapproval

Our Town Vocabulary Juggle Letters 2

1. NOLSCGIW = 1. _____
   Frowning in anger or disapproval

2. SSUBLNUGRSIUOE = 2. _____
   Gloominess; ridiculously dismal

3. OAHPESHPT = 3. _____
   Soda fountain drink with carbonated water & flavored syrup

4. EEWNDA = 4. _____
   Slowly detached from something one is used to having

5. EARLENT = 5. _____
   Lasting forever

6. HDAUGEISN = 6. _____
   Agonized; tormented

7. CNLSAAD = 7. _____
   Incident that brings about disgrace or offends society

8. INGIDELT = 8. _____
   Marked by persevering, painstaking effort

9. FTNESELCARL = 9. _____
   Dejected; dispirited or depressed

10. UBRAPTLY =10. _____
    In a short or brusque manner

11. CVNROPSEI =11. _____
    Areas situated away from the population center

12. IDNFEINETRF =12. _____
    Having no particular interest or concern for

13. RFFODTENA =13. _____
    Intentionally insulted

14. RBAENR =14. _____
    Empty; bare

15. RDOCUBK =15. _____
    Prickly, weed-like plant with purple flower

Our Town Vocabulary Juggle Letters 2 Answer Key

1. NOLSCGIW = 1. SCOWLING
   Frowning in anger or disapproval

2. SSUBLNUGRSIUOE = 2. LUGUBRIOUSNESS
   Gloominess; ridiculously dismal

3. OAHPESHPT = 3. PHOSPHATE
   Soda fountain drink with carbonated water & flavored syrup

4. EEWNDA = 4. WEANED
   Slowly detached from something one is used to having

5. EARLENT = 5. ETERNAL
   Lasting forever

6. HDAUGEISN = 6. ANGUISHED
   Agonized; tormented

7. CNLSAAD = 7. SCANDAL
   Incident that brings about disgrace or offends society

8. INGIDELT = 8. DILIGENT
   Marked by persevering, painstaking effort

9. FTNESELCARL = 9. CRESTFALLEN
   Dejected; dispirited or depressed

10. UBRAPTLY = 10. ABRUPTLY
    In a short or brusque manner

11. CVNROPSEI = 11. PROVINCES
    Areas situated away from the population center

12. IDNFEINETRF = 12. INDIFFERENT
    Having no particular interest or concern for

13. RFFODTENA = 13. AFFRONTED
    Intentionally insulted

14. RBAENR = 14. BARREN
    Empty; bare

15. RDOCUBK = 15. BURDOCK
    Prickly, weed-like plant with purple flower

Our Town Vocabulary Juggle Letters 3

1. ICENCOTED = 1. _____
   Vain; holding an unusually high opinion of oneself

2. GINDLITE = 2. _____
   Marked by persevering, painstaking effort

3. CASANDL = 3. _____
   Incident that brings about disgrace or offends society

4. IBNLYGIT = 4. _____
   In a nasty way intending to hurt someone

5. REVSOPCNI = 5. _____
   Areas situated away from the population center

6. BATUEAL = 6. _____
   Interlude during a scene when all performers freeze momentarily

7. NDSIUGEAH = 7. _____
   Agonized; tormented

8. PEHLROTIEO = 8. _____
   Flowers native to Peru, having fragrant, purple flowers

9. EEEARDBV = 9. _____
   Suffering from the loss of a loved one

10. STOHEPAPH =10. _____
    Soda fountain drink with carbonated water & flavored syrup

11. RUEBLG =11. _____
    Steal

12. NCRVGIITNO =12. _____
    Planning with cleverness or ingenuity

13. ENTFNRFEIID =13. _____
    Having no particular interest or concern for

14. DFFTROENA =14. _____
    Intentionally insulted

15. UPRLTBYA =15. _____
    In a short or brusque manner

Our Town Vocabulary Juggle Letters 3 Answer Key

1. ICENCOTED = 1. CONCEITED
   Vain; holding an unusually high opinion of oneself

2. GINDLITE = 2. DILIGENT
   Marked by persevering, painstaking effort

3. CASANDL = 3. SCANDAL
   Incident that brings about disgrace or offends society

4. IBNLYGIT = 4. BITINGLY
   In a nasty way intending to hurt someone

5. REVSOPCNI = 5. PROVINCES
   Areas situated away from the population center

6. BATUEAL = 6. TABLEAU
   Interlude during a scene when all performers freeze momentarily

7. NDSIUGEAH = 7. ANGUISHED
   Agonized; tormented

8. PEHLROTIEO = 8. HELIOTROPE
   Flowers native to Peru, having fragrant, purple flowers

9. EEEARDBV = 9. BEREAVED
   Suffering from the loss of a loved one

10. STOHEPAPH = 10. PHOSPHATE
    Soda fountain drink with carbonated water & flavored syrup

11. RUEBLG = 11. BURGLE
    Steal

12. NCRVGIITNO = 12. CONTRIVING
    Planning with cleverness or ingenuity

13. ENTFNRFEIID = 13. INDIFFERENT
    Having no particular interest or concern for

14. DFFTROENA = 14. AFFRONTED
    Intentionally insulted

15. UPRLTBYA = 15. ABRUPTLY
    In a short or brusque manner

Copyrighted

Our Town Vocabulary Juggle Letters 4

1. INYIGTLB = 1. _____
In a nasty way intending to hurt someone

2. SPOARXENAIET = 2. _____
Feeling of impatient anger or annoyance

3. RIEOHLEPTO = 3. _____
Flowers native to Peru, having fragrant, purple flowers

4. ASLNCDA = 4. _____
Incident that brings about disgrace or offends society

5. YCLGEA = 5. _____
Something handed down from an ancestor

6. LGIENDIT = 6. _____
Marked by persevering, painstaking effort

7. NOLICGSW = 7. _____
Frowning in anger or disapproval

8. DERBAVEE = 8. _____
Suffering from the loss of a loved one

9. IADESNGHU = 9. _____
Agonized; tormented

10. EENTLRA =10. _____
Lasting forever

11. TIRGNNVIOC =11. _____
Planning with cleverness or ingenuity

12. PEOATHSPH =12. _____
Soda fountain drink with carbonated water & flavored syrup

13. PLBTAUYR =13. _____
In a short or brusque manner

14. JEINUTCSI =14. _____
Violation of another's rights or of what is right

15. AEDNEW =15. _____
Slowly detached from something one is used to having

Our Town Vocabulary Juggle Letters 4 Answer Key

1. INYIGTLB = 1. BITINGLY
   In a nasty way intending to hurt someone

2. SPOARXENAIET = 2. EXASPERATION
   Feeling of impatient anger or annoyance

3. RIEOHLEPTO = 3. HELIOTROPE
   Flowers native to Peru, having fragrant, purple flowers

4. ASLNCDA = 4. SCANDAL
   Incident that brings about disgrace or offends society

5. YCLGEA = 5. LEGACY
   Something handed down from an ancestor

6. LGIENDIT = 6. DILIGENT
   Marked by persevering, painstaking effort

7. NOLICGSW = 7. SCOWLING
   Frowning in anger or disapproval

8. DERBAVEE = 8. BEREAVED
   Suffering from the loss of a loved one

9. IADESNGHU = 9. ANGUISHED
   Agonized; tormented

10. EENTLRA =10. ETERNAL
    Lasting forever

11. TIRGNNVIOC =11. CONTRIVING
    Planning with cleverness or ingenuity

12. PEOATHSPH =12. PHOSPHATE
    Soda fountain drink with carbonated water & flavored syrup

13. PLBTAUYR =13. ABRUPTLY
    In a short or brusque manner

14. JEINUTCSI =14. INJUSTICE
    Violation of another's rights or of what is right

15. AEDNEW =15. WEANED
    Slowly detached from something one is used to having

ABRUPTLY	In a short or brusque manner
AFFRONTED	Intentionally insulted
ANGUISHED	Agonized; tormented
BARREN	Empty; bare
BEREAVED	Suffering from the loss of a loved one
BITINGLY	In a nasty way intending to hurt someone

BURDOCK	Prickly, weed-like plant with purple flower
BURGLE	Steal
CONCEITED	Vain; holding an unusually high opinion of oneself
CONTRIVING	Planning with cleverness or ingenuity
CRESTFALLEN	Dejected; dispirited or depressed
DILIGENT	Marked by persevering, painstaking effort

ETERNAL	Lasting forever
EXASPERATION	Feeling of impatient anger or annoyance
GOSSIPING	Spreading rumors or talk of a personal or sensational nature
HELIOTROPE	Flowers native to Peru, having fragrant, purple flowers
INDIFFERENT	Having no particular interest or concern for
INJUSTICE	Violation of another's rights or of what is right

LEGACY	Something handed down from an ancestor
LUGUBRIOUSNESS	Gloominess; ridiculously dismal
PHOSPHATE	Soda fountain drink with carbonated water & flavored syrup
PROSCENIUM	Stage area between curtain and orchestra
PROVINCES	Areas situated away from the population center
SCANDAL	Incident that brings about disgrace or offends society

SCOWLING	Frowning in anger or disapproval
TABLEAU	Interlude during a scene when all performers freeze momentarily
WEANED	Slowly detached from something one is used to having

Our Town Vocabulary

INJUSTICE	PROSCENIUM	CONCEITED	BARREN	TABLEAU
AFFRONTED	INDIFFERENT	CRESTFALLEN	EXASPERATION	WEANED
SCANDAL	GOSSIPING	FREE SPACE	PROVINCES	SCOWLING
ABRUPTLY	HELIOTROPE	CONTRIVING	BURGLE	LUGUBRIOUSNESS
PHOSPHATE	ETERNAL	ANGUISHED	BURDOCK	LEGACY

Our Town Vocabulary

BEREAVED	BITINGLY	LEGACY	BURDOCK	ANGUISHED
ETERNAL	PHOSPHATE	LUGUBRIOUSNESS	BURGLE	CONTRIVING
HELIOTROPE	ABRUPTLY	FREE SPACE	PROVINCES	DILIGENT
GOSSIPING	SCANDAL	WEANED	EXASPERATION	CRESTFALLEN
INDIFFERENT	AFFRONTED	TABLEAU	BARREN	CONCEITED

Our Town Vocabulary

CONTRIVING	GOSSIPING	INJUSTICE	BURGLE	ETERNAL
BURDOCK	CONCEITED	ABRUPTLY	DILIGENT	EXASPERATION
LEGACY	PROSCENIUM	FREE SPACE	BITINGLY	ANGUISHED
SCANDAL	BEREAVED	CRESTFALLEN	PHOSPHATE	INDIFFERENT
BARREN	SCOWLING	PROVINCES	LUGUBRIOUSNESS	WEANED

Our Town Vocabulary

TABLEAU	AFFRONTED	WEANED	LUGUBRIOUSNESS	PROVINCES
SCOWLING	BARREN	INDIFFERENT	PHOSPHATE	CRESTFALLEN
BEREAVED	SCANDAL	FREE SPACE	BITINGLY	HELIOTROPE
PROSCENIUM	LEGACY	EXASPERATION	DILIGENT	ABRUPTLY
CONCEITED	BURDOCK	ETERNAL	BURGLE	INJUSTICE

Our Town Vocabulary

AFFRONTED	CONCEITED	BITINGLY	EXASPERATION	INDIFFERENT
LEGACY	CRESTFALLEN	BURGLE	HELIOTROPE	BEREAVED
DILIGENT	GOSSIPING	FREE SPACE	BURDOCK	SCANDAL
WEANED	TABLEAU	ABRUPTLY	INJUSTICE	PHOSPHATE
SCOWLING	ETERNAL	PROVINCES	LUGUBRIOUSNESS	CONTRIVING

Our Town Vocabulary

BARREN	ANGUISHED	CONTRIVING	LUGUBRIOUSNESS	PROVINCES
ETERNAL	SCOWLING	PHOSPHATE	INJUSTICE	ABRUPTLY
TABLEAU	WEANED	FREE SPACE	BURDOCK	PROSCENIUM
GOSSIPING	DILIGENT	BEREAVED	HELIOTROPE	BURGLE
CRESTFALLEN	LEGACY	INDIFFERENT	EXASPERATION	BITINGLY

Our Town Vocabulary

PHOSPHATE	ETERNAL	SCANDAL	BURDOCK	BITINGLY
HELIOTROPE	SCOWLING	ANGUISHED	DILIGENT	PROSCENIUM
CONCEITED	BARREN	FREE SPACE	CONTRIVING	WEANED
LUGUBRIOUSNESS	LEGACY	AFFRONTED	BEREAVED	INDIFFERENT
GOSSIPING	CRESTFALLEN	PROVINCES	BURGLE	INJUSTICE

Our Town Vocabulary

ABRUPTLY	TABLEAU	INJUSTICE	BURGLE	PROVINCES
CRESTFALLEN	GOSSIPING	INDIFFERENT	BEREAVED	AFFRONTED
LEGACY	LUGUBRIOUSNESS	FREE SPACE	CONTRIVING	EXASPERATION
BARREN	CONCEITED	PROSCENIUM	DILIGENT	ANGUISHED
SCOWLING	HELIOTROPE	BITINGLY	BURDOCK	SCANDAL

Our Town Vocabulary

CONTRIVING	ETERNAL	ANGUISHED	EXASPERATION	BURDOCK
LEGACY	CRESTFALLEN	HELIOTROPE	PROVINCES	INDIFFERENT
BARREN	ABRUPTLY	FREE SPACE	AFFRONTED	CONCEITED
SCOWLING	GOSSIPING	DILIGENT	WEANED	LUGUBRIOUSNESS
PHOSPHATE	SCANDAL	BURGLE	BEREAVED	TABLEAU

Our Town Vocabulary

INJUSTICE	PROSCENIUM	TABLEAU	BEREAVED	BURGLE
SCANDAL	PHOSPHATE	LUGUBRIOUSNESS	WEANED	DILIGENT
GOSSIPING	SCOWLING	FREE SPACE	AFFRONTED	BITINGLY
ABRUPTLY	BARREN	INDIFFERENT	PROVINCES	HELIOTROPE
CRESTFALLEN	LEGACY	BURDOCK	EXASPERATION	ANGUISHED

Our Town Vocabulary

BURGLE	GOSSIPING	ABRUPTLY	LUGUBRIOUSNESS	TABLEAU
LEGACY	BITINGLY	INJUSTICE	CONTRIVING	DILIGENT
SCANDAL	BARREN	FREE SPACE	ANGUISHED	AFFRONTED
EXASPERATION	BURDOCK	CRESTFALLEN	WEANED	INDIFFERENT
PROVINCES	PROSCENIUM	HELIOTROPE	PHOSPHATE	CONCEITED

Our Town Vocabulary

BEREAVED	SCOWLING	CONCEITED	PHOSPHATE	HELIOTROPE
PROSCENIUM	PROVINCES	INDIFFERENT	WEANED	CRESTFALLEN
BURDOCK	EXASPERATION	FREE SPACE	ANGUISHED	ETERNAL
BARREN	SCANDAL	DILIGENT	CONTRIVING	INJUSTICE
BITINGLY	LEGACY	TABLEAU	LUGUBRIOUSNESS	ABRUPTLY

Our Town Vocabulary

BITINGLY	BEREAVED	PHOSPHATE	SCANDAL	INJUSTICE
CONCEITED	AFFRONTED	HELIOTROPE	LUGUBRIOUSNESS	BARREN
BURGLE	SCOWLING	FREE SPACE	TABLEAU	PROSCENIUM
ETERNAL	DILIGENT	WEANED	CONTRIVING	ABRUPTLY
INDIFFERENT	PROVINCES	CRESTFALLEN	EXASPERATION	GOSSIPING

Our Town Vocabulary

BURDOCK	ANGUISHED	GOSSIPING	EXASPERATION	CRESTFALLEN
PROVINCES	INDIFFERENT	ABRUPTLY	CONTRIVING	WEANED
DILIGENT	ETERNAL	FREE SPACE	TABLEAU	LEGACY
SCOWLING	BURGLE	BARREN	LUGUBRIOUSNESS	HELIOTROPE
AFFRONTED	CONCEITED	INJUSTICE	SCANDAL	PHOSPHATE

Our Town Vocabulary

CONTRIVING	GOSSIPING	TABLEAU	INDIFFERENT	DILIGENT
LUGUBRIOUSNESS	BURGLE	CRESTFALLEN	BARREN	INJUSTICE
ANGUISHED	BURDOCK	FREE SPACE	CONCEITED	PROVINCES
SCANDAL	BEREAVED	EXASPERATION	BITINGLY	AFFRONTED
HELIOTROPE	LEGACY	SCOWLING	ABRUPTLY	ETERNAL

Our Town Vocabulary

PHOSPHATE	WEANED	ETERNAL	ABRUPTLY	SCOWLING
LEGACY	HELIOTROPE	AFFRONTED	BITINGLY	EXASPERATION
BEREAVED	SCANDAL	FREE SPACE	CONCEITED	PROSCENIUM
BURDOCK	ANGUISHED	INJUSTICE	BARREN	CRESTFALLEN
BURGLE	LUGUBRIOUSNESS	DILIGENT	INDIFFERENT	TABLEAU

Our Town Vocabulary

DILIGENT	EXASPERATION	WEANED	INDIFFERENT	BURGLE
HELIOTROPE	PHOSPHATE	ETERNAL	ABRUPTLY	PROVINCES
AFFRONTED	GOSSIPING	FREE SPACE	BITINGLY	LUGUBRIOUSNESS
PROSCENIUM	BEREAVED	CONCEITED	BARREN	SCANDAL
ANGUISHED	CONTRIVING	LEGACY	TABLEAU	INJUSTICE

Our Town Vocabulary

SCOWLING	CRESTFALLEN	INJUSTICE	TABLEAU	LEGACY
CONTRIVING	ANGUISHED	SCANDAL	BARREN	CONCEITED
BEREAVED	PROSCENIUM	FREE SPACE	BITINGLY	BURDOCK
GOSSIPING	AFFRONTED	PROVINCES	ABRUPTLY	ETERNAL
PHOSPHATE	HELIOTROPE	BURGLE	INDIFFERENT	WEANED

Our Town Vocabulary

ETERNAL	GOSSIPING	PROVINCES	TABLEAU	EXASPERATION
BURGLE	PHOSPHATE	AFFRONTED	BURDOCK	BITINGLY
INDIFFERENT	INJUSTICE	FREE SPACE	SCANDAL	BARREN
ABRUPTLY	BEREAVED	DILIGENT	HELIOTROPE	PROSCENIUM
WEANED	ANGUISHED	SCOWLING	LEGACY	CONCEITED

Our Town Vocabulary

CRESTFALLEN	LUGUBRIOUSNESS	CONCEITED	LEGACY	SCOWLING
ANGUISHED	WEANED	PROSCENIUM	HELIOTROPE	DILIGENT
BEREAVED	ABRUPTLY	FREE SPACE	SCANDAL	CONTRIVING
INJUSTICE	INDIFFERENT	BITINGLY	BURDOCK	AFFRONTED
PHOSPHATE	BURGLE	EXASPERATION	TABLEAU	PROVINCES

Our Town Vocabulary

CRESTFALLEN	PHOSPHATE	BURDOCK	SCOWLING	EXASPERATION
BURGLE	PROSCENIUM	LUGUBRIOUSNESS	LEGACY	BARREN
BEREAVED	ABRUPTLY	FREE SPACE	TABLEAU	CONTRIVING
WEANED	BITINGLY	ANGUISHED	INDIFFERENT	HELIOTROPE
ETERNAL	PROVINCES	SCANDAL	INJUSTICE	AFFRONTED

Our Town Vocabulary

DILIGENT	GOSSIPING	AFFRONTED	INJUSTICE	SCANDAL
PROVINCES	ETERNAL	HELIOTROPE	INDIFFERENT	ANGUISHED
BITINGLY	WEANED	FREE SPACE	TABLEAU	CONCEITED
ABRUPTLY	BEREAVED	BARREN	LEGACY	LUGUBRIOUSNESS
PROSCENIUM	BURGLE	EXASPERATION	SCOWLING	BURDOCK

Our Town Vocabulary

SCOWLING	BARREN	PROSCENIUM	CONCEITED	PHOSPHATE
ABRUPTLY	ETERNAL	DILIGENT	INDIFFERENT	BURDOCK
TABLEAU	LUGUBRIOUSNESS	FREE SPACE	GOSSIPING	BITINGLY
WEANED	INJUSTICE	CRESTFALLEN	PROVINCES	EXASPERATION
BURGLE	AFFRONTED	ANGUISHED	HELIOTROPE	SCANDAL

Our Town Vocabulary

LEGACY	CONTRIVING	SCANDAL	HELIOTROPE	ANGUISHED
AFFRONTED	BURGLE	EXASPERATION	PROVINCES	CRESTFALLEN
INJUSTICE	WEANED	FREE SPACE	GOSSIPING	BEREAVED
LUGUBRIOUSNESS	TABLEAU	BURDOCK	INDIFFERENT	DILIGENT
ETERNAL	ABRUPTLY	PHOSPHATE	CONCEITED	PROSCENIUM

Our Town Vocabulary

PROVINCES	BURGLE	TABLEAU	EXASPERATION	DILIGENT
HELIOTROPE	ETERNAL	BITINGLY	SCANDAL	ANGUISHED
BURDOCK	INJUSTICE	FREE SPACE	WEANED	INDIFFERENT
AFFRONTED	BARREN	PHOSPHATE	CONCEITED	SCOWLING
ABRUPTLY	PROSCENIUM	BEREAVED	GOSSIPING	CONTRIVING

Our Town Vocabulary

CRESTFALLEN	LEGACY	CONTRIVING	GOSSIPING	BEREAVED
PROSCENIUM	ABRUPTLY	SCOWLING	CONCEITED	PHOSPHATE
BARREN	AFFRONTED	FREE SPACE	WEANED	LUGUBRIOUSNESS
INJUSTICE	BURDOCK	ANGUISHED	SCANDAL	BITINGLY
ETERNAL	HELIOTROPE	DILIGENT	EXASPERATION	TABLEAU

Our Town Vocabulary

INDIFFERENT	SCANDAL	ANGUISHED	CRESTFALLEN	SCOWLING
INJUSTICE	BURDOCK	TABLEAU	AFFRONTED	BARREN
GOSSIPING	PHOSPHATE	FREE SPACE	EXASPERATION	DILIGENT
CONCEITED	BITINGLY	LEGACY	PROSCENIUM	HELIOTROPE
WEANED	LUGUBRIOUSNESS	BURGLE	ETERNAL	BEREAVED

Our Town Vocabulary

ABRUPTLY	CONTRIVING	BEREAVED	ETERNAL	BURGLE
LUGUBRIOUSNESS	WEANED	HELIOTROPE	PROSCENIUM	LEGACY
BITINGLY	CONCEITED	FREE SPACE	EXASPERATION	PROVINCES
PHOSPHATE	GOSSIPING	BARREN	AFFRONTED	TABLEAU
BURDOCK	INJUSTICE	SCOWLING	CRESTFALLEN	ANGUISHED

Our Town Vocabulary

BURGLE	WEANED	PHOSPHATE	CONTRIVING	SCOWLING
HELIOTROPE	DILIGENT	BARREN	AFFRONTED	PROSCENIUM
BEREAVED	BITINGLY	FREE SPACE	GOSSIPING	ABRUPTLY
BURDOCK	EXASPERATION	CONCEITED	ETERNAL	LUGUBRIOUSNESS
SCANDAL	ANGUISHED	CRESTFALLEN	INJUSTICE	PROVINCES

Our Town Vocabulary

INDIFFERENT	TABLEAU	PROVINCES	INJUSTICE	CRESTFALLEN
ANGUISHED	SCANDAL	LUGUBRIOUSNESS	ETERNAL	CONCEITED
EXASPERATION	BURDOCK	FREE SPACE	GOSSIPING	LEGACY
BITINGLY	BEREAVED	PROSCENIUM	AFFRONTED	BARREN
DILIGENT	HELIOTROPE	SCOWLING	CONTRIVING	PHOSPHATE

Our Town Vocabulary

INDIFFERENT	PHOSPHATE	BARREN	CONCEITED	ABRUPTLY
BEREAVED	ANGUISHED	HELIOTROPE	LEGACY	ETERNAL
LUGUBRIOUSNESS	WEANED	FREE SPACE	BURGLE	GOSSIPING
SCOWLING	DILIGENT	PROSCENIUM	INJUSTICE	SCANDAL
PROVINCES	CONTRIVING	AFFRONTED	CRESTFALLEN	TABLEAU

Our Town Vocabulary

BURDOCK	BITINGLY	TABLEAU	CRESTFALLEN	AFFRONTED
CONTRIVING	PROVINCES	SCANDAL	INJUSTICE	PROSCENIUM
DILIGENT	SCOWLING	FREE SPACE	BURGLE	EXASPERATION
WEANED	LUGUBRIOUSNESS	ETERNAL	LEGACY	HELIOTROPE
ANGUISHED	BEREAVED	ABRUPTLY	CONCEITED	BARREN

www.ingramcontent.com/pod-product-compliance
Lightning Source LLC
Chambersburg PA
CBHW081458070526
44586CB00019B/2409